BestMasters

Springer awards „BestMasters“ to the best master’s theses which have been completed at renowned universities in Germany, Austria, and Switzerland.
The studies received highest marks and were recommended for publication by supervisors. They address current issues from various fields of research in natural sciences, psychology, technology, and economics.
The series addresses practitioners as well as scientists and, in particular, offers guidance for early stage researchers.

Florian Auinger

The Causal Relationship between the S&P 500 and the VIX Index

Critical Analysis of Financial Market Volatility and Its Predictability

Springer Gabler

Florian Auinger
Linz, Austria

BestMasters
ISBN 978-3-658-08968-9 ISBN 978-3-658-08969-6 (eBook)
DOI 10.1007/978-3-658-08969-6

Library of Congress Control Number: 2015932842

Springer Gabler

Printed on acid-free paper

Springer Gabler is a brand of Springer Fachmedien Wiesbaden
Springer Fachmedien Wiesbaden is part of Springer Science+Business Media
(www.springer.com)

List of Acronyms and Abbreviations

Bps	Basis points
BSM	Black and Scholes Model (Black-Scholes Theorem)
BF	Behavioural Finance
CAPM	Capital Asset Pricing Model
CFE	Chicago Futures Exchange
CBOE	Chicago Boards Option Exchange
CSFB	Credit Suisse Fear Barometer
dcv	Daily Close Value
EMH	Efficient Market Hypothesis
ETPs	Exchange Traded Products
FED	Federal Reserve Bank
IV	Implied Volatility
OEX	Standard & Poor's 100 Index
SPX	Standard & Poor's 500 Index
VDAX	German Volatility Index
VIX	CBOE Volatility Index

List of Figures

List of Tables

List of Equations

1 Introduction

Financial volatility enjoys increasing relevance in risk managers' daily business. According to the fifth annual survey of emerging risks, carried out in 2012 by the Society of Actuaries, Casualty Actuarial Society and the Canadian Institute of Actuaries, financial volatility was cited as the highest emerging risk with 68% of the respondents declaring it as one of their top three concerns (Ladd 2012). Another research highlighting the importance of volatility risk management was conducted by the Association of Corporate Treasurers and Barclays in 2012. The study reports the management views and practices of more than 100 treasury chiefs coming from a wide range of industries in the United Kingdom, the rest of Europe, the Middle East, Africa, Asia-Pacific and North America. The results show that the reduction of earnings volatility is one of the top three risk management objectives for 92% of the respondents and for 41% of the participants it is even the top risk management priority (Sawers 2012). These surveys are just a small sample of studies that demonstrate the enormous relevance of volatility management for financial professionals.

Consequently, understanding and predicting future market volatility is a fundamental desire for researchers and practitioners as it is highly relevant for decision making in several areas, such as security valuation, investment, risk management, monetary policy making, etc. To be specific, volatility is often used as a crude measure of the total risk of financial assets and hence, forecasts of stock market volatility are fundamental in the timing of investment decisions (Majmudar and Banerjee 2004, Chen 1997). Moreover, the expected future volatility plays an essential role in the risk assessment of portfolios and is an important input in portfolio selection models and dynamic diversification techniques (Blenman and Wang 2012, Chen 1997). Additionally, a measure of volatility is important in the derivative securities pricing theory and a key input in the pricing of contingent claims such as stock options. When pricing stock options for instance, a forecast of the future volatility of the underlying asset is needed for the time period until option expiry (Chen 1997). In addition, there are also instruments that offer a direct exposure to volatility as an investment, including derivative products such as variance swaps, forward variance swaps and VIX futures. As a consequence, accurate predictions are once again necessary to offer the investor the potential to make more direct profit (Warren 2012). In summary, with regards to the high relevance of this topic for practitioners and the various applications where volatility is a fundamental input, how to accurately predict or at least estimate future volatility is crucial in many financial decision-making situations.

1.1 Problem Statement

In order to provide a benchmark of expected short-term market volatility, the Chicago Board Options Exchange (CBOE) introduced the VIX Index in 1993 (Whaley 2008). According to some researchers such as Nwogugu (2012), however, the VIX is not only inaccurate and inefficient, but it is also based on an incorrect and misleading formula of computation consequently resulting in a biased VIX level. Other scientists indicate that volatility predictability in general may be scrutinized, because it is highly dependent on factors such as, for instance, the data frequency and the chosen forecasting horizon and hence decays quickly with an increasing time frame (Christoffersen and Diebold 2000). To date, much has been studied on the correlation between the SPX (Standard & Poor's 500 Index) and the VIX Index and has been well documented in academic journals. There has also been a great deal of research focusing on the analysis of the VIX and its derivative products, but regarding the causation of the SPX and the VIX Index and the related opportunity of index forecastability, a very limited amount of research has been carried out. In other words, there are many open questions concerning the controversies within research regarding the critical analysis of the VIX Index, volatility forecasting and the causation of the SPX and/or the VIX Index.

1.2 Research Objective

In consideration of the critical opinions about volatility prediction and the VIX Index mentioned above, the purpose of the literature review of this research paper is to analyse the weaknesses and sources of criticism concerning volatility forecasting and in particular the VIX Index. Furthermore, the influence of behavioural finance (hereinafter BF) on financial market volatility will be examined. The empirical analysis of this research paper aims to contribute to the existing literature about the VIX Index and volatility predictability by investigating the causation of the SPX and the VIX, of which very limited research exists. Moreover, the aim is to analyse whether there is any difference between the causal relationship in times of economic booms and recessions. In doing so, three research questions will be answered in this master thesis. Firstly, the causal relationship will be addressed in order to clarify whether the SPX Granger causes the VIX Index and/or vice-versa. Secondly, the predictability of the future movements of the SPX and the VIX will be examined and finally, the contradictions and similarities regarding volatility management and forecasting between theory and practice will be discussed. The result of this is a research gap being closed in various dimensions, including index causation, volatility forecastability and behavioral influence.

1.3 Research Structure

The literature review has been organized as follows: first, the theoretical dimensions of this research will be laid out, with a focus on risk and emotions and on financial market volatility. In doing so, the questions of the real definition of volatility, whether it can be predicted at all and how it can be measured are going to be answered by reviewing the existing literature. Regarding the forecastability of future volatility, the research of Christoffersen and Diebold (2000), in which they analysed the appropriate time horizon for volatility prediction, will be of importance. In addition, various volatility measures and forecasting models will be analysed concerning their predictive abilities, mainly by referring to Poon and Granger (2003), whose research is well-known in this regard. In the second part, the influence of behavioural finance on price movements and financial market volatility will be analysed in order to assess, whether volatility is exclusively rooted in rational behaviour, as is stated in the Efficient Market Hypothesis (hereinafter EMH), or whether prices are also influenced by the emotionality of market participants. In discussing these aspects, the academic works of Olsen (1998), Shiller (2003), Zouaoui, Nouyrigat and Beer (2011) and Howard (2013) will be highly relevant. In the next part, this research paper will give a brief overview of the VIX Index, its history, the purpose behind the introduction, the computation formula and its various applications in practice. Moreover, some strategies of VIX application will be presented and critical opinions about the VIX's historical performance will be addressed.

Regarding the empirical part of this research paper, both a quantitative and a qualitative analysis have been included. Thereby, a triangulation of empirical methods and an opportunity to cross-check research results is established. In the beginning, there will be a descriptive analysis with the aim of exploring the normal distribution of the data to assess the need for data transformation regarding the skewness and kurtosis levels. Next, the correlation between the SPX and the VIX Index will be proven. The causal relationship between the two indexes will then be analysed by conducting a Granger's test for causality in order to examine whether the SPX Granger causes the VIX Index and/or vice-versa. In doing so, the dependence of the index causality on the current state of the economy (recession or boom) will also be explored. Using the causal relationship obtained, the predictability of the future index movement (direction and/or extent) of the SPX and/or the VIX will be assessed. Following this, the propositions derived from the literature review and the findings of the quantitative research part are discussed in semi-structured interviews with financial market experts. Finally, the last section concludes the paper with a summary of the research findings, a discussion of these findings in order to reflect them theoretically and the conclusion. In addition, the limits of this study and potential opportunities for further research will be presented in the conclusion of this master thesis.

2 Methodology

The formulation and logic of the appropriate research design were based on the objectives of this research paper and the associated research questions presented in the introduction of this paper. The following chapter provides an overview of the research process and, therefore, starts with a general description of the procedure, followed by more detailed information regarding the empirical analysis in the subsequent subchapters.

2.1 Research Design

In general, methodological fit is a key criterion to ensure the quality of research and consequently, it is also highly relevant for this research paper. The literature review has shown that there are many studies covering the topic of volatility forecasting and the VIX Index in particular. Not only are there a high number of serious academic works on the topic, but also the fact that the constructs and concepts studied over time are well-developed allows the conclusion to be drawn that the current state of literature is perceived to be mature. A mature theory implies that research questions tend to focus on clarifying and elaborating existing concepts within a growing body of interrelated theories (Edmondson and McManus 2007). Since the status of literature is interpreted as being mature, already existing theories are examined deductively by applying theory to data. Traditionally, the deductive approach illustrated in Figure 1 goes hand in hand with a quantitative research method, but in this master thesis mixed methods are applied by integrating quantitative and qualitative data within one research project, an approach which is increasingly used and accepted (Bryman 2012). In doing so, a greater confidence in research findings will be achieved through triangulation, which was defined rather broadly by Denzin (1970) as an approach that uses multiple observers, sources of data, theoretical perspectives, methodologies, etc. Increasingly, however, the term triangulation is also used to refer to a process of cross-checking the research findings derived from quantitative and qualitative research (Deacon and Fenton 1998).

After reviewing the existing literature, the process of deduction continues with the formulation of the research hypothesis. The hypothesis and the process of data collection are described in chapter 2.3 and 2.4 of this research. Next, the research findings from both quantitative and qualitative analysis are presented in chapter 7 and the answers to the research questions and the confirmation or rejection of the related hypothesis are included in chapter 8. Finally, the theoretical reflection of the obtained findings concludes the research process illustrated in Figure 1 (see the discussion in chapter 8 for further information).

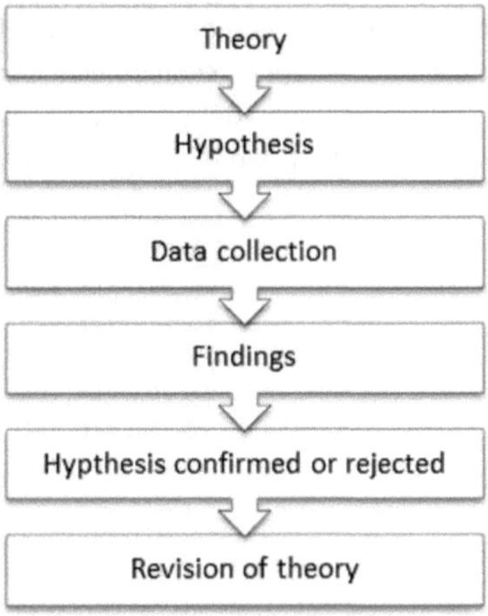

Figure 1: Process of deduction

2.2 Literature Review

The literature review is a key step in all research in order to determine all aspects which should be considered, namely what is already known about the topic and what kind of controversies exist. Furthermore, it also allows the researcher to link the research questions and hypothesis to the existing literature and consequently, is an important component for demonstrating the credibility and contribution of the research to existing studies (Bryman 2012). In doing so, the context of this research, namely risk management, volatility forecasting, the VIX Index and the influence of behavioral finance has always been a major consideration.

Source of Information	Examples
Electronic databases	SSRN, EBSCO, Wiley, acm, Emerald, etc.
Websites	CBOE website, yahoo.finance,etc.
Search engines	google scholar, google, google books, etc.
Specialised books	e.g. Social Research methods (Bryman)
Video channels	Youtube

Table 1: Sources of information (own table)

Table 1 gives some examples of the sources of information being used to search for relevant journal articles, index quotes, website content, specialised books, figures, tables, etc. It should be mentioned that the video channel Youtube was explicitly used in order to become familiar with data treatment and data analysis using SPSS. In addition, Figure 2 shows the main topics that were covered within the literature review.

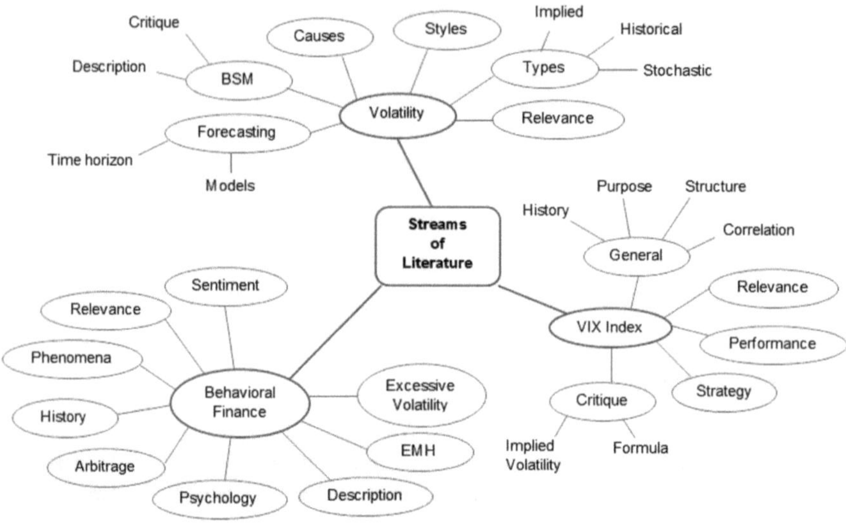

Figure 2: Streams of literature

2.3 Quantitative Research

In order to answer the question whether the SPX Granger causes the VIX and whether this is a reciprocal relationship, the relevant variables (daily changes of the SPX and VIX) were analysed statistically. The process of quantitative research is shown in Figure 3 and starts with the task of data preparation. The data sample used consists of the daily log-returns calculated from the daily close values of the S&P 500 Index and the VIX Index. Unfortunately, high-frequency data such as hourly or minute-by-minute quotes was not easily available and probably costly to collect leading to the focus in this research being explicitly on daily returns. Furthermore, the time horizon was divided into three sections in order to avoid bias through crisis-related index tendencies. The first section covers the period of economic upturn from 2003 to 2006, the second covers the recent financial crisis between 2007 and 2008 when the SPX dropped significantly and finally, the third section ranges from 2009 until 2013. This distinction makes it possible to show potential differences between the causal relationship of the SPX and the VIX during periods of economic growth and recession. After downloading the relevant data from the Yahoo Finance Website, the log-returns were calculated in Excel for the relevant time periods in order to prepare the data for further analysis. In total the sample size consists of 2,766 observations, whereby time period one covers 1,008 observations, period two covers 504 observations and finally, the most recent period consists of 1,254 observations. The sample size of 2,766 daily returns and an observation time frame of eleven years makes it possible to draw the conclusion that research results fulfil the stability criteria and that there is no fluctuation of research results (Bryman 2012). As a consequence, the assumed stability of research findings indicates that all elements of the quantitative research, including the descriptive analysis and the Granger causality test, are reliable.

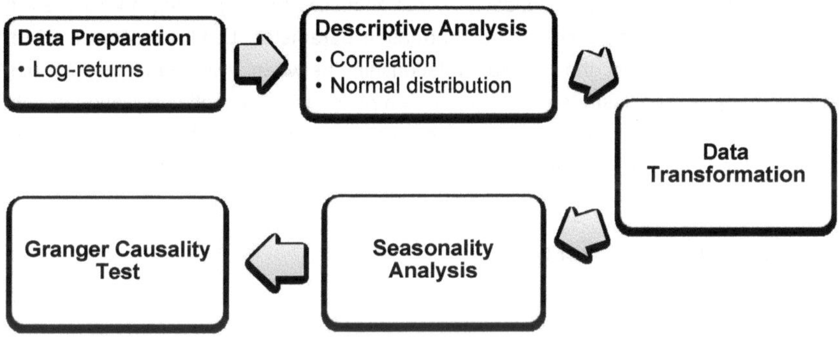

Figure 3: Quantitative research process (own figure)

The data preparation was followed by the next step of the quantitative research, namely the descriptive analysis of the time series. Firstly, although the correlation between the SPX and the VIX Index has already been proven by various pieces of research, the correlation analysis is supposed to be an introductory step of the quantitative study. SPSS was used for both, the analysis regarding normal distribution of the data set and for the correlation analysis. Next, it was assessed whether the data set is normally distributed and consequently, the necessity of data transformation procedures to adjust skewness and kurtosis was also appraised. In order to evaluate the fulfilment of the normal distribution assumption, the following criteria were formulated for the skewness and kurtosis levels of the log-returns.

Normal Distribution Criteria	
Normal Distribution	**Non-normal Distribution**
[-1 ≤ Skewness ≤ +1]	[- ∞ < Skewness < -1]; [+1 < Skewness < ∞]
2 x Std.Error > Skewness	2 x Std.Error < Skewness
2 x Std.Error > Kurtosis	2 x Std.Error < Kurtosis

Table 2: Normal distribution criteria (own table)

Assessing the degree of normal distribution is also critical because one of the major inputs in the "Bivariate Granger Causality – Free Statistics Software", which was used for the causal analysis, is the Box-Cox transformation parameter "Lambda" (Wessa 2013). This software computes the causal relationship between two variables in both directions. Figure 4 illustrates the input template of this software and all the necessary inputs. The following list serves as a description of these inputs and explains the applied procedure to find the appropriate variables.

2.3.1 Granger Causality Test Input:

- **Data X (SPX)**
  - Log returns of daily close values (dcv) + constant value c

    $= \ln (dcv_{(t)} / dcv_{(t-1)}) + c$

- **Data Y (VIX)**
  - Log returns of daily close values (dcv) + constant value c

    $= \ln (dcv_{(t)} / dcv_{(t-1)}) + c$

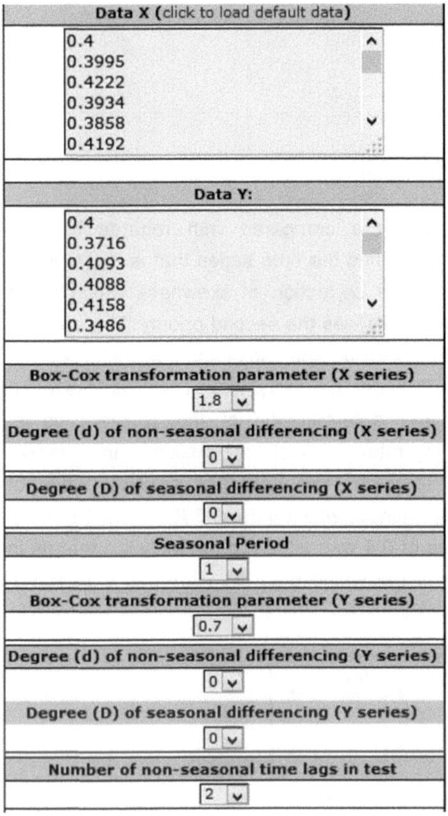

Figure 4: Input layout of Granger causality test software (Wessa 2013)

- **Box-Cox transformation parameter (X and Y series)**

In order to find the appropriate Box-Cox transformation parameter for each variable in every period, the following procedure was applied. First, the data series were transformed using the formula presented in Equation 1. It should be noted that the first formula was used for all values smaller or greater than zero, whereas the second was used for Lambda equalling zero. Due to the fact that the "Bivariate Granger Causality – Free Statistics Software" only allows the transformation parameter to range between -2 and +2 with one decimal interval, the original data was Box-Cox transformed using each possible Lambda parameter, amounting to 41 transformations.

$$y^{(\lambda)} = \begin{cases} \dfrac{y^{\lambda}-1}{\lambda} & (\lambda \neq 0), \\ \log y & (\lambda = 0), \end{cases}$$

Equation 1: Box-Cox transformation parameter formula

As a next step, all 41 time series were compared with regards to their level of skewness and kurtosis in order to find the time series that is most similar to a normal distribution. In doing so, the correction of skewness was chosen to be the top priority and kurtosis adjustment was the second priority. The Lambda value of this time series was later used as the Box-Cox parameter of the particular index and period for the Granger causality test. There is, however, another step in between, namely the determination of the constant value. This is necessary because the log-returns must be positive and hence, the constant value "c" was added to them. Therefore, the smallest value of all SPX and VIX log-returns was determined, which was -0.3650 (See Table 3). As a consequence, the constant value of 0.4 was added to the daily log-returns in order to ensure positive values across the whole data set (Box and Cox 1964).

Descriptive Statistics

	N	Minimum	Maximum
SPX (2003-2013)	2766	-,0947	,1096
VIX (2003-2013)	2766	-,3506	,4960
Valid N (listwise)	2766		

Table 3: Minimum and maximum value of SPX & VIX

Figure 5 shows the most appropriate Lambdas that were determined by applying the criterion presented in Table 2. These Lambdas were then used as the Box-Cox transformation parameters for the Granger causality test (See the appendix for all SPSS outputs).

Optimal Lamdas						
			Skew		Kurtosis	
	Time Period	Lamda	Statistic	Std. Error	Statistic	Std. Error
SPX	2003-2006	1,8	-0,673	0,077	-0,764	0,154
	2007-2008	1,7	0,410	0,077	9,387	0,154
	2009-2013	1,7	0,089	0,069	1,915	0,138
VIX	2003-2006	0,7	0,134	0,077	3,750	0,154
	2007-2008	0,7	0,200	0,109	3,176	0,217
	2009-2013	0,6	0,078	0,069	4,605	0,138

Figure 5: Most appropriate lambda values (own table)

- **Degree of non-seasonal (d) and seasonal differencing (D) for SPX**

In order to detect any potential seasonal pattern of the S&P 500 Index that could affect the Granger causality test, its daily log-returns were analysed from January 2003. In Figure 6 you can see that especially between 2003 and 2007, the daily changes of the SPX stayed within a very narrow range of +/- 4%, followed by a more volatile period caused by the financial crisis. Since 2012 however, the situation is obviously the way it was before the economic recession without any major trends. In other words, the opportunity of spikes in the log-returns is definitely given and can be triggered by events such as global financial recessions. However, such developments are difficult to foresee and are not considered to be either seasonal nor stable over time.

As a consequence, the assumption can be made that there is no significant seasonal pattern in the log-returns of the S&P 500 Index. Hence, the degree of non-seasonal and seasonal differencing was kept stable with an input value of zero throughout all periods.

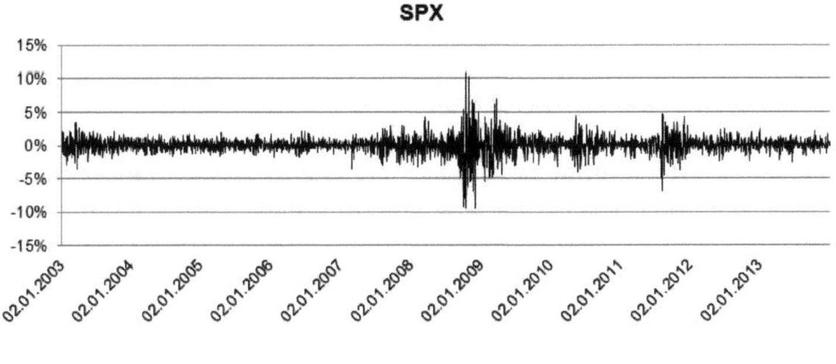

Figure 6: Daily returns SPX 2003 - 2013 (own Figure)

- **Degree of non-seasonal (d) and seasonal differencing (D) for VIX**

  Similar to the procedure for the SPX that was mentioned above, the seasonality was also analysed for the VIX Index over the same time period. A first look at Figure 7 shows that in general, the range within the VIX Index fluctuates is definitely larger compared with the SPX. But there is no seasonal patter observable in the VIX. Consequently, the assumption that no seasonal effect is incorporated can also be derived for the daily changes of the VIX Index. Therefore, the degree of non-seasonal and seasonal differencing was kept constant for the VIX as well with an input value of zero.

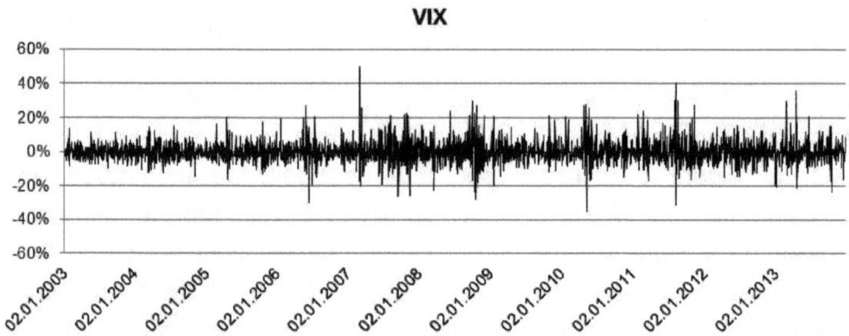

Figure 7: Daily returns VIX 2003 - 2013 (own Figure)

Due to the fact that the data set explicitly consists of daily close values, potential data structure phenomena like, for instance, intraday seasonality were not considered.

- **Seasonal Period**

  Due to the fact that there is no significant seasonal pattern observable, the value for the seasonal period is always 1.

- **Number of non-seasonal time lags in test**

  In order to test the decay of causality and forecastability, Granger causality was computed for each time lag that was possible to enter in the software, ranging from 1 to 11 lags.

The results obtained by using this software will provide answers to the research question of SPX and VIX Index causation and, therefore, help to confirm or reject the formulated hypothesis:

RQ 1: ***What is the causal relationship: Does the VIX Granger cause the S&P 500 movement or vice-versa?***

In order to answer this research question, the following hypotheses have been formulated and derived from the literature review. In doing so, the level of statistical significance that is acceptable was $p < 5\%$, which implies that there are fewer than 5 chances in 100 observations that there could be a Granger causality relationship between the two variables (Bryman 2012):

H_0: The VIX Index does not Granger cause the S&P 500 index.

A null hypothesis stipulates that two variables are not related. In this respect, that would mean that the VIX Index cannot be used to forecast the SPX movement because there is no Granger causal relationship (Bryman 2012). For both situations, rejecting and confirming H_0, the alternative hypotheses H_A and H_B have been formulated:

H_A: The VIX Index Granger causes the S&P 500 Index.

As is mentioned in chapter 6.1, the VIX Index is also called "Investor Fear Gauge", because in general, a high level of the VIX is related to a high level of fear among investors, whereas a low VIX level is associated with complacency (CBOE 2014c). Furthermore, Howard (2013) has shown that emotional crowds dominate market pricing and volatility and they drive prices based on the latest scenarios, whether optimistic or pessimistic. These facts lead to the argumentation that SPX investors observe the level of the VIX Index and thereby, the level of fear in the market when deciding to buy, hold or sell stocks. As a consequence, any significant change in the VIX Index results in certain behaviour of SPX investors. In the case of a sharp VIX increase, traders will rush to sell their assets, whereas in the case of a sharp VIX decline, traders will buy or at least hold their SPX stocks. This allows the formulation of the alternative hypothesis H_A as stated above.

H_B: The S&P 500 Index Granger causes the VIX Index.

The second alternative hypothesis H_B claims the exact opposite of H_A. In chapter 6.3 there is a presentation of the main sources of criticism regarding the VIX Index and its predictive performance. According to a study by Laszlo Birinyi and Kevin Pleines, which was presented in the Seattle Times, the VIX is just a coincidental indicator with limited predictive value and consequently all but useless for forecasting the direction of equity prices. Moreover, it is argued that the VIX measures the volatility of the market today, but not tomorrow or the day after and is supposed to have little connection to future equity prices. Instead, Birinyi and Pleines claim that the VIX Index moves in lock-step with stock prices (Kisling 2010). These opinions allow us to draw the assumption that the S&P 500 Index Granger causes the VIX Index and, consequently the alternative hypothesis H_B was formulated based on these arguments.

In general, by confirming or rejecting H_A you cannot automatically answer H_B, because if H_A is true, H_B could, but not necessarily has to, be true as well. On the contrary, if H_A is rejected, H_B could, but must not necessarily, be confirmed. In other words, both alternative hypotheses will only be confirmed if the causal relationship between the SPX and the VIX Index is found to be reciprocal.

Furthermore, a sub-question was derived from the research question defined above that is formulated as follows:

RQ 2: ***(Given the findings obtained by answering RQ 1)***
Are the future changes of the S&P 500 and/or the VIX predictable?

The answer to this sub-question is mainly based on the outcomes of the causal relationship analysis examined by the first research question. The obtained quantitative research findings are presented within chapter 7, including the answers to all research questions and the rejection or acceptance of the hypotheses.

2.4 Qualitative Research

The objective of the qualitative research was to assess the contradictions and similarities between the existing theory regarding volatility management and forecasting and the practical perspective. In doing so, the obtained findings from the literature review and the Granger causality test were discussed and reflected upon with the help of bank industry experts. Thereby, the following qualitative research question was addressed:

RQ 3: ***What are the main contradictions and similarities between volatility forecasting and volatility management in theory and practice?***

In order to discuss the results from the literature review and the quantitative research findings but nevertheless offer the participating experts a high level of flexibility in answering questions, semi-structured interviews were conducted. Furthermore, due to the fact that this research method is rather flexible, the interviewee and the interviewer had a great deal of freedom when following the interview guide. In order to find proper interview partners, a purposive sampling process was undertaken. First, the type of industry where interview partners are supposed to be employed was chosen, namely the Austrian bank industry. For reasons of accessibility of interviewees and the opportunity to talk personally with them, the sample was limited to Austrian participants. Next, portfolio management, risk management and fund management were defined as the appropriate departments from which the experts should come. As was already mentioned in the introduction, estimating or at least a judging future market volatility is critical in those finance jobs and consequently, interview partners from these departments were deemed to be the appropriate contact persons for providing additional information from a practical perspective. Finally, the attributes that should characterize interview partners were specified, including sufficient work experience and know-how in their business. In conclusion, the sampling process can be divided into two sections, namely the so-called “sampling of context” by choosing the relevant industry and department, followed by the “sampling of participants” by defining the adequate attributes (Bryman 2012). As a result, the three participating interview partners who fulfilled the sampling criteria came from two different Austrian banks. Unfortunately, none wanted their name and institution to be mentioned in this research paper and consequently, this information has been kept anonymous. Two interviewees are fund managers and the third is a portfolio manager for individual clients and as a result, they are all frequently engaged in buying and selling equities, options, etc.

As already mentioned, the research question addresses potential contradictions and similarities between theory and practice and thus, the main topics discussed in the interviews were the following: first, the relevance of the VIX in financial decision-making and potential alternatives instead of the VIX was discussed; second, the awareness regarding the critique of the VIX Index was assessed and the question whether volatility options and futures are traded was examined. Finally, the influence and relevance of behavioural finance, the adequate time horizon for volatility estimation and the causal relationship between the VIX and the SPX was addressed.

When analysing the outcomes of qualitative interviews, coding is considered to be a crucial task. A code is very often just a single word or a short phrase that symbolically assigns a summative and essence-capturing attribute for a portion of language-based data such as interview transcripts in this case. Next, similarly coded data was grouped and organized in categories that share the same characteristics, accompanied by a steady process of recoding and re-categorizing of codes. Finally, the “reality” was transcended of the data and progressed toward the theoretical and conceptual (Saldaña 2012). The obtained outcomes are presented in chapter 7.2 and in order to find more information regarding the dimension, categories and codes derived from the semi-structured interviews, the coding template has been included and can be seen in the appendix of this paper.

As already mentioned earlier, this research can be divided into a three-step-process of literature review, quantitative data analysis and qualitative information collection from industry experts. Figure 8 illustrates the research design of this study graphically and shows the three steps and their main characteristics, through which triangulation is established and cross-checking enabled.

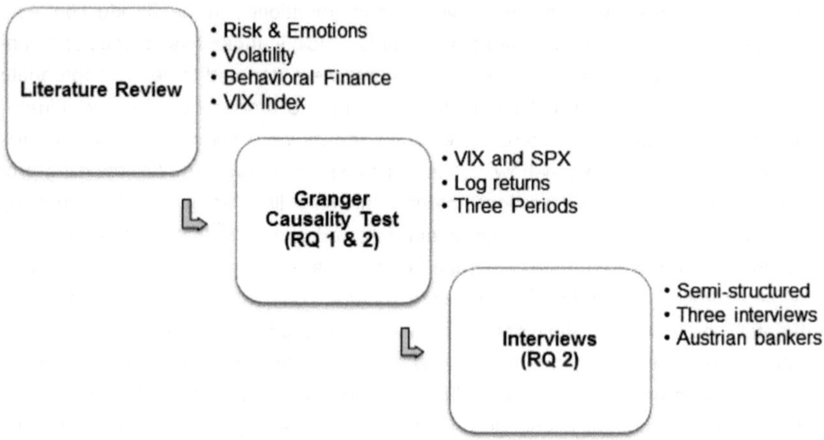

Figure 8: Research design (own Figure)

3 Risk and Emotions

Due to the fact that the target groups of this research paper are financial risk managers and investment brokers, to start with a short introduction covering risk management topics would be useful. However, this chapter is not meant to provide a collection of definitions and differences between risk and uncertainty or systemic and systematic risk. The author is aware of the fact that the readers of this research paper already have this knowledge and, therefore, this part follows another objective. The aim of this section is to give an overview of the topics that have been recently discussed regarding risk and uncertainty and in doing so, establish a link to another major topic of this master thesis, namely behavioral finance.

Existing neuroeconomics evidence shows that the same brain areas that process information about risk, rewards and punishments are also involved in generating emotional states. As a result, it would also be meaningful to shed light on the interdependencies between these two issues (Kuhnen and Knutson 2011). In general, human judgements, opinions and impressions are fashioned by one's background, professional experience and personal understanding. Therefore, risks can be perceived differently by every individual based on the way they see or feel toward the potential danger. In addition, it is well demonstrated in research that many factors influence a person's risk perception. Furthermore, some research findings indicated that perceived risk plays a more important role than actual risk within the decision-making process (Ricciardi 2008).

There are a number of studies that examined the influence of emotions and a person's emotional state when making decisions. Cavalheiro et al. (2011), demonstrate that individuals with a positive mood were more tolerant towards risk and explained that relationship by supposing that in moments of positive mood, people are less critical about their decisions. This may lead us to make decisions with little previous analysis. Most interestingly, no significant difference between men and women was found in their study. These findings were confirmed by Kuhnen and Knutson (2011), who concluded that situations associated with positive and arousing emotions such as, for instance, excitement lead to riskier decisions, whereas those associated with negative and arousing emotions such as anxiety result in more risk-averse choices. This can be explained by a person's increased confidence in the ability to evaluate risky investments which is released by positive affect. But Kuhnen and Knutson (2011) also point out that the participants of their study had to make fast decisions in an experimental setting and therefore, the results could differ when people have much more time to deliberate and make financial choices. Although these research results are maybe influenced by its limitations, there is another study that indicates that risk tolerance is at least to a certain degree a function of a person's current affective state. Grable and Roszkowski (2008), report that being in euphoric mood when making decisions could result in an overestimation of an investor's typical risk tolerance level. On the contrary, however, negative emotional state is not necessarily associated with a low level of risk tolerance. Durand, Simon and Szimayer (2009), demonstrated that high-arousal-based moods including anger and stress can lead to increased risk-seeking, whereas low-arousal-based negative moods such as sadness and depression elicit non-biased and systematic information processing that can be interpreted as either passive or rational. In other words, negative emotions that are often experienced during bear regimes not always result in risk-averse behaviour because investors appear to require a higher return to compensate them for their exposure to a variety of risk dimensions. Another interesting fact concerning risk assessment was studied by Loewenstein et al. (2001), who analysed how people react when making decisions under risky conditions. In general, people react to risk at two levels. Firstly, they evaluate the risk cognitively and secondly, they react to it emotionally. These two reactions are interrelated, but people often fear a discrepancy between the fear they experience in connection with a certain risk and their cognitive evaluation of the threat posed by that risk.

In conclusion, various studies have shown that there is a clear relationship between emotions and the level of risk tolerance of investors. Whereas there is a strong tendency to higher risk tolerance when emotions are rather positive and optimistic, this must not necessarily be the case. It may also be the case that investors response to negative emotions and higher risk levels by taking even more risks in order to achieve the expected returns. Due to the fact that emotions play an essential role in financial decision-making, this topic is present in various parts of this work such as chapter 5 which covers a discussion regarding behavioral finance and the Efficient Market Hypothesis. Furthermore, the influence of behavioral aspects will also be investigated within the qualitative analysis of the empirical research.

4 Financial Market Volatility

The aim of the following chapter is to provide an overview of the basics about volatility management and forecasting. This chapter is therefore structured in the following way: as the relevant and importance of volatility forecasts is already highlighted, first it is necessary to clarify what exactly is meant by the term volatility and where it has its roots in order to clarify the scope of this research paper. Moreover, a collection of different opinions about the predictability of future volatility is also provided, followed by a comparison of the predictive ability of various volatility types, including realized, model and implied volatility and associated models.

4.1 Current Trends and Latest News

This chapter is the outcome of a simple search engine request in order to collect information about the main topics that are recently discussed in newspapers. In doing so, the focus was placed on current developments concerning volatility and the VIX Index.

According to Yahoo.Finance (2014), this year will be a year of volatility in contrast to 2013. In general, volatility on stock exchanges is heavily influenced by the monetary policies of central banks, such as the Federal Reserve Bank (FED) or the European Central Bank. After six years of quantitative easing, 2014 is supposed to be a year of transition. It is very probable that investors are already anticipating higher interest rates but nevertheless, they react nervously after news announcements about a possible end of low interest rates. Traders worry that as soon as the FED lowers interest rates, the state of the economy will deteriorate as then it would be more expensive for businesses and individuals to borrow money, causing a cut in corporate profits and spending. Another interesting statement was issued by BMO Capital Markets strategist Brian Belski, who argued that periods of increased volatility were going to inevitably coincide with any change in direction from the FED, because for the past 15 years an entire generation of investors has built careers around the notion that the FED and low interest rates drive stock markets and not fundamentals. Nevertheless, it must be mentioned that rising interest rates do not mean danger for stock markets because according to most economist, the US economy will improve over the course of this current year and next and consequently, companies will be aided in improving their profits. To sum this up, the monetary policies of central banks is an important psychological factor and as interest rates will probably increase, traders should at least expect volatility to also increase.

Apart from investigating the world's largest economy, it is always interesting to take a look at "developing" countries such as the emerging countries. Therefore, the CBOE Emerging Markets Exchange Traded Fund (hereinafter ETF) Volatility (VXEEM) is very useful. It tracks volatility in emerging markets companies and was up more than 20% this year due to worries about the economic developments in these markets. For the upcoming months it will be of interest to observe volatility in these markets and the VXEEM in particular (Solomon 2014). Besides, a recent survey of global fund managers by the Bank of America Merrill Lynch showed that investors worldwide worried most about geopolitical tensions, the situation of the financial markets in China and the expected weak earnings in emerging markets (Yahoo.Finance 2014).

During the search for news and information in the internet it was considered to be of interest to collect a few pieces of advices and recommendations given by so-called "experts", including analysts, investors, fund managers, etc. The following recommendations could well be made to someone asking for advice regarding developments on financial markets:

- Current periods of high volatility are a buying opportunity,
- Increase your exposure to high-quality and larger-cap names that tend to have better chance of withstanding periods of market stress,
- Even if volatility is does not matter for you if you have a long-term orientation with your investments. More money has been lost by market timing than with market fluctuations.
- Go abroad! US stocks are near all-time highs, but in the emerging markets for instance, stocks have declined over the past three years and are at the lower end of their valuation spectrum.
- There are a few asset classes that could offer protection during a volatile period for equities, such as cash and uncorrelated alternative investments (Solomon 2014), (Bilello 2014).
- Although the current level of the VIX Index is comparatively low, some experts warn that this could just be a house of cards as the price of insuring against market instability is not a good predictor (Officer 2009).

By comparing the preceding paragraph about the survey that uncovered worries about emerging markets and the penultimate bullet-point, it can be observed that on the one hand, advices should always be regarded with suspicion irrespective of the advisor. On the other hand, it can be naive to rely on surveys and research that promise to predict a certain trend in financial markets. Finally, with regards to the last piece of advice, it seems that there are "experts" that have doubts about the predictive ability of the VIX Index. The next paragraph concerns two current newspaper articles that establish a link between the current volatility situation and behavioural finance.

In an online newspaper article the author refers to the psychological aspect of human overreaction, which is often a driver of volatility in financial markets. In addition, the abundance of financial information together with low transaction costs has made it easier for investors to react quickly to market events over the last decades. Negative news can cause traders to sell a certain stock only to see it rise again the following day. On January 13th 2014 for example, the SPX fell by 1.26% as investors reacted to an FED official hinting at additional tapering. The next day however, the index rose again by 1.08% without material news, but fortunately, overreactions by a certain group of investors can create predictable and exploitable opportunities for others (Libertini 2014). The other newspaper article focuses on sentiment as opposed to overreaction and refers to the Investors Intelligence Sentiment Poll, which is a collection of forecasts by investor newsletter writers. This poll states that whereas in March 2009, the bears outnumbered the bulls by over 20%, in 2014 the situation had been completely reversed, namely that the bulls outnumbered the bears by over 45%. According to the author of the newspaper article, this is an important fact to monitor because at sentiment extremes, the market often moves in the opposite direction of the crows. This would mean that forward returns are expected to be weak (Bilello 2014).

The aim of this chapter was to give the reader an impression of the current trends, rumours and advices in financial newspapers and on webpages. It should be considered, however, that some of the studies and surveys mentioned are probably not totally representative and that some of these studies and surveys were conducted with a clear objective, namely presenting results that are useful to their personal and institutions' needs. Nevertheless, it was deemed interesting to also consider such opinions, because obviously many market participants trust in them and listen to such streams of information.

4.2 Definitions, Sources and Measures of Volatility

There are various alternatives to define volatility, including mathematical and non-mathematical definitions. Concerning the latter, volatility can be defined as the tendency for prices to change with respect to new information regarding the value of the underlying asset or due to the demand for liquidity by impatient traders (Harris 2002). Poon (2005), explains volatility as the spreads of all likely outcomes of an uncertain variable. With regards to the mathematical definitions, a variable's volatility is often defined as the standard deviation (σ) of the return. This is provided by the variable per unit of time when the return is expressed using continuous compounding, whereby the unit of time can vary depending on the practical application. For instance, whereas for risk management purposes the unit of time is usually one day, it can also be one year when volatility is used as an input for option pricing (Hull 2012). Risk managers often focus on the variance rate instead of volatility, which is the squared standard deviation given by equation (1):

(1) $$\hat{\sigma}^2 = \frac{1}{N-1}\sum_{i=1}^{N}(R_i - \bar{R})^2$$

where R_i is the close-to-close return on the market index at date i, $\bar{R}$ is the mean stock market return over the period of observation, and N corresponds to the number of data points used in the calculations (Turner and Weigel 1992). Due to the fact that variance is simply the squared standard deviation, it makes no difference which measure is used when comparing various assets. On the one hand, it must be considered that the variance is less stable and less desirable than standard deviation as an object of volatility forecasting evaluation and computer estimation. Furthermore, mean and standard deviation have the same unit of measure for instance, if the mean is mean is measured in dollars then the standard deviation is also expressed in dollars. Variance on the contrary would be measured in dollar squared. Therefore, it makes sense to use standard deviation when thinking about volatility (Poon 2005). On the other hand, the standard deviation of stock returns is not always a good indicator of variability because typically it is calculated using closing prices. In doing so, price changes throughout the trading day are ignored and a volatility estimate using standard deviation is an approximation but is not exact. Due to the compounding effect, the dispersion of investment returns conforms to a log-normal instead of a normal distribution and hence, results in an inexact estimate (Kritzman 1991). In addition, the typical standard deviation gives more weight to larger daily changes because of the squaring of the observations (Daigler and Rossi 2006). Finally, standard deviation is only a measure for the spread of a distribution and, therefore, includes no information on its shape as long as the observations are not normally distributed. This is another argument for the denial of standard deviation as a good or perfect measure of risk (Poon 2005).

However, despite the classical way of measuring financial market volatility by calculating sample standard deviation, Gençay et al. (2001) distinguish between three main types of volatility measurements, namely realized, model and implied volatility:

- **Realized volatility:** is also called “historical volatility” because it is determined by past observations;

- **Model volatility:** is a virtual variable in a theoretical model like for instance GARCH or stochastic volatility but there may be a means to calculate this variable from data; and finally,

- **Implied volatility:** is the approach of using reported option prices to infer volatility expectations. In other words, the implied volatility (hereinafter IV) should accurately reflect the forecasted volatility of the underlying asset over the remaining investment period of the option (Blenman and Wang 2012).

In chapter 4.5 there is a detailed description of each of these volatility types, including a discussion of their main weaknesses.

Concerning the sources of financial market volatility, French and Roll (1986) indicate that volatility is caused by new information. Additionally, however, they differentiate between public and private information. Whereas public information is information that becomes public at the same time as it affects stock prices, private information only affects prices through trading. These two sources of financial market volatility might help to explain the fact that according to French and Roll's study, there is an enormous difference between volatility during exchange trading hours and non-trading hours. In detail, their study shows that the return variance per hour was approximately 70 times larger during a trading day hour than during a weekend non-trading hour, over all stocks listed on the New York and American Exchanges between 1963 and 1982. They consider three factors that might explain this phenomenon: first, public information may be more frequent during trading days; second, private information may be more likely to affect prices when exchanges are open and finally, the process of trading itself may induce volatility. Although, this research is obviously rather old, the findings are still assumed to be relevant nowadays. Bondt and Thaler (1985), and De Bondt and Thaler (1987) for instance, found out that individuals do not only react to no new information but they even overreact to new information. In accordance, Kahneman and Tversky (1973) have shown that individuals overestimate current information and underestimate more distant news when revising their expectations. These might be first signs of behavioural influence in financial decision-making. Besides the fact that the release of new information may cause volatility, it can also come from mispricing. According to French and Roll (1986), on average, approximately 4 to 12% of the daily variance is caused by mispricing. To sum up, it can be said that there are many sources that may explain stock price movements. Among them, volatility can be caused by varying fundamentals, mispricing, by the release of new information, by behavioural aspects of market participants, etc. Concerning the latter, there will be a detailed discussion about efficient markets and behavioural finance in chapter 5.

4.3 Volatility Characteristics and Stylized Facts

The following chapter covering volatility characteristics and stylized facts should provide a collection of explanations which may prove useful for reading and understanding parts of this research paper.

In research, it is common to divide the historical development of volatility into sections, so-called volatility regimes. The empirical results of Baba and Sakurai (2011) have shown that during the 1990-2010 period three volatility regimes are identifiable, namely tranquil regimes characterised by low volatility, turmoil regimes with high volatility levels and crisis regimes with extremely high volatility levels. Furthermore, it was found that the probability of regime-switching from the tranquil to the turmoil regime is significantly influenced by lower term spreads. In order to investigate the effect of macroeconomic variables such as the term spread on regime shifts, the Markov regime-switching approach was utilized. Additionally, they assume that the crisis regime is characterised by the highest level of standard deviation and of the VIX Index (Baba and Sakurai 2011).

Another stylized fact about volatility is that stock prices, as already proposed by Press (1967), are not normally distributed. One explanation, therefore, is that prices are hit by occasional shocks, also called "jumps", which cause temporary departures from normality. A discussion on the jump component of the S&P 500 volatility and the ability of the VIX to capture current and future jumps will be provided at a later stage of this work. Additionally, studies of frequency distribution of individual stock prices beginning as early as Fama (1965) show that the distribution of changes in the logarithm of stock prices has fat tails. In other words, the relative frequency of large changes is greater than for the normal distribution. Furthermore, the distribution is leptokurtic, meaning that it is more bundled in the middle than normal distribution. The fat tail phenomenon has also been used to describe another stylized fact, namely the volatility smile (Fortune 1996). Volatility smile is a term for explaining the non-linear shape of implied volatility plots (Majmudar and Banerjee 2004).

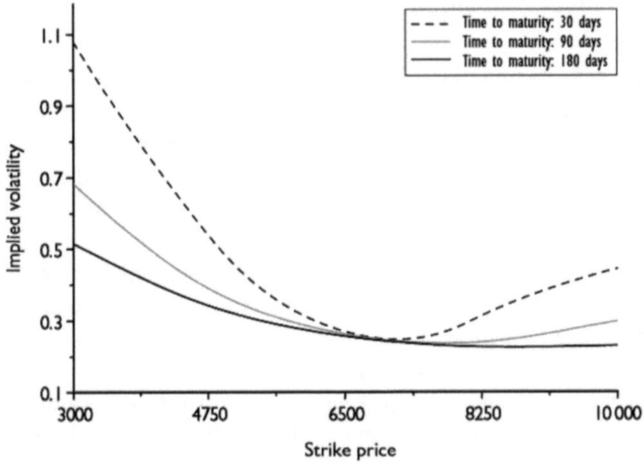

Figure 9: Volatility smiles for options with 30, 90 and 180 days to maturity

The volatility smile explains the fact that options far out of or far in the money have higher implied volatilities than near-the-money options, as is illustrated in Figure 9 (Fortune 1996). Another stylized fact is that volatility is assumed to be mean-reverting, meaning that periods of high volatility tend to be followed by a period of low volatility and, vice-versa, a period of low volatility will be followed by a rise in volatility (Majmudar and Banerjee 2004). Studies that document that the VIX swings back in the opposite direction after great changes include Toikka et al. (2004) & Rattray and Balasubramanian (2003). In addition, "volatility clustering" is a term based on the fact that long periods of high volatility are often interspersed by periods of relative calm (Majmudar and Banerjee 2004).

Another volatility phenomenon is the volatility paradox. It describes the tendency that endogenous risk does not go away as exogenous risk decreases. This is the case because as the exogenous risk falls, the system becomes more prone to volatility spikes and the financial system spends more time in a crisis state where capital is misallocated (Brunnermeier and Sannikov 2012). In other words, times of low volatility tend to be associated with an increase of leverage, which in consequence increases future systemic risk. With regards to the VIX Index, higher levels of the VIX tend to precede declines in leverage. In other words, there is a negative correlation between volatility and expected leverage growth (Adrian and Boyarchenko 2012).

4.4 Predictability of Future Volatility

In general, the success and accuracy of any prediction of a future development, no matter whether we are talking about forecasting the weather or the future stock movement, definitely depends greatly on the defined time horizon. But what is the adequate time horizon for risk management? To address this question there must be a distinction between the various tasks and applications in the area of risk management, because obviously, there is no one-fits-all time horizon. Whereas Smithson and Minton (1996) note that almost all risk managers use a one-day risk management approach for trading purposes, Falloon (1999) argues that for investors, the appropriate time horizon is approximately one year and for pension funds it may be as long as even ten years. Poon and Granger (2003), agree that volatility is definitely forecastable, but the debate is on how far ahead the future volatility level and future volatility changes can be predicted. According to Bollerslev, Chou and Kroner (1992), future volatility is definitely forecastable on a very high frequency basis, like, for instance, hourly or daily.

Christoffersen and Diebold (2000), tried to answer the question of the appropriate time horizon and the decay of volatility forecast accuracy as the relevant time horizon increases and if this decay does indeed occur, after how many hours, days, weeks or even years its process starts or accelerates. They conclude that the forecastability of future volatility can vary not only on the chosen horizon, but also with the assumed model. As a consequence, they developed a model-free procedure for assessing volatility forecastability across time horizons in global foreign exchange, bond and stock markets. Due to the fact that this research focuses on the relationship between the VIX Index and the S&P 500 index, explicitly the results regarding the forecastability in stock markets will be presented. The outcomes of the authors indicate that for horizons of less than ten trading days, equity return volatility is significantly forecastable and conversely for time horizons greater than ten trading days. However, Christoffersen and Diebold (2000) tested both the forecastability of future volatility, but also the strength of the former. For very short time periods between one and ten trading days, the strength of forecastability is significant, but decreases quickly and consistently. As soon as the time horizon reaches approximately ten days or often even before, the strength is statistically insignificant, indicating that volatility forecastability has vanished (Christoffersen and Diebold 2000).

4.5 Volatility Types

In the following sub-chapters there is a brief presentation of the main volatility types, namely implied, realized and stochastic/model volatility, followed by a comparison of each of them.

4.5.1 Implied Volatility

Implied volatility emerges from daily option trading activities and measures to what extent the returns of the underlying asset fluctuate from the current date until option expiry (Cipollini and Manzini 2007). In other words, if option markets are efficient and pricing models correct, then the implied volatilities should equal the forecasted volatility of the asset over the remaining life of the option (Blenman and Wang 2012). On the one hand, a decline in implied volatility indicates complacency and on the other hand, an increase is associated with fear in the stock markets. Whereas implied volatility is directly linked to option prices, the connection to the underlying stock is non-linear and consequently, difficult to investigate. In general, the relation between IV and the underlying stock asset can be explained by the fact that an increase in implied volatility is the result of a rise in options' prices, which could be associated with the demand to hedge equity risk (Cipollini and Manzini 2007). One method to calculate implied volatilities is the Black and Scholes Model or Black-Scholes theorem (hereinafter BSM). This model is an important concept in modern financial theory and is considered the standard model for valuing options (Yalincak 2012). The BSM uses a number of inputs to determine the value of an option, including the current stock price, the risk-free interest rate, time to option maturity, exercise price and volatility of returns. Despite the latter, all parameters included in the formula are known in advance. Therefore, the volatility is derived by a backward induction, resulting in the already mentioned "implied volatility" (Majmudar and Banerjee 2004). Providing a continuous dividend is paid at a constant rate, the BSM applies directly to European options. In the case of no dividend payments, the BSM also applies to American CALL options, which can be exercised at any time. However, the model does not apply to any American option (put or call) when a dividend is paid, nor does it hold for American PUT options, because these might be exercised early (Fortune 1996).

On the one hand, the strengths of the BSM are incontestable and one of these strengths is rooted in the possibility to estimate market volatility of an underlying as a function of price and time without direct reference to risk aversion measures, expected yield or utility functions. In addition, the self-replicating strategy, enabling traders to theoretically and continuously buy and sell derivatives by the strategy and never incur losses, is another strong argument in favour of the Black-Scholes theorem. But on the other hand, however, its shortcomings have become increasingly clear over the last three decades and most of the criticism refers to counterfactual assumptions on which the model is based: the BSM assumes that asset prices follow a random walk, but this assumption does not hold as stock prices are determined by several factors that cannot be assigned the same probability in the way they will affect the movement of stock prices. Moreover, the Black-Scholes theorem assumes volatility to be constant, but at least since 1987, this assumption has proven false. In fact, volatility can be constant in the short-term, but it can never be constant in the long-term, because the volatility level fluctuates over time. In addition, the phenomenon of volatility clustering, which was explained earlier, is another argument against constant volatility Yalinçak (2012). More information with regards to the constant volatility assumption will be provided in chapter 6.3.1. The BSM also assumes that interest rates are constant, that stocks do not pay dividends and that there are no commissions and transactions costs such as taxes. The assumptions mentioned above can also be declared as being unrealistic. First, interest rates do change in times of increased volatility. Second, the absence of dividend payments does not apply in the case of most of the stock assets and finally, the absence of fees for buying and selling options and stocks is hardly the case in any financial market. According to the Black and Scholes model, financial markets are supposed to be perfectly liquid. In other words, it should be possible to purchase and sell any amount of stocks or options at any given time. Unfortunately, the events of 1987, 1998 and 2007-2008 show that markets are not perfectly liquid (Yalincak 2012). Another assumption the BSM makes is that traders will eliminate any arbitrage opportunities by simultaneously buying (or writing) options and writing (or buying) the option-replicating portfolio whenever profitable opportunities appear. In doing so, they force option, stock and bond prices to conform to an equilibrium relationship (Fortune 1996). Unfortunately, though there are limits to arbitrage that make it impossible or at least costly for traders to utilize arbitrage opportunities in reality, as you can read in chapter 5.2 which is about the critical opinions concerning the Efficient Markets Hypothesis. Nevertheless, despite the shortcomings of the BSM mentioned above, the model still remains in wide-spread use. Shu and Zhang (2003), examined the so-called "Heston Model" which is supposed to be an alternative for the BSM, but their research findings show that the IV computed from BSM has higher explanatory power than that computed from the Heston Model. As a consequence, no further discussion regarding the Heston Model is included in this research.

During the description of the volatility types and specifically the BSM, there was much criticism included regarding the assumptions on which it is based. In general, however, there is no one-size-fits-all model that cures every problem, because not every aspect of the market can be considered in any given model, as each factor affecting the price of a stock or an option cannot be captured mathematically. Consequently, mathematical models can only attempt to capture most of the aspects and refer to their limitations (Yalincak 2012). Moreover, every theory requires assumptions that might be considered unrealistic, but if the focus is placed exclusively on criticizing the underlying assumptions, it is likely that there will be no foundations for deriving the generalizations that make theories useful. Finally, the only proper test of a theory is to evaluate its predictive ability regardless of the assumptions required to generate it, the one that consistently predicts best is the best theory (Fortune 1996).

4.5.2 Realized Volatility

Another wide-spread approach for estimating future volatility of financial assets is to use time series techniques and past behaviours of assets prices to infer a future trend. Consequently, such an approach using post behaviour to project the future is backward looking (Blenman and Wang 2012). Some methods to use realized volatility to forecast future volatility are presented in the next chapter. Shu and Zhang (2003), examined how the method to measure realized volatility affects the relationship between realized and implied volatilities. In doing so, they tested four different realized volatility estimators. First, there is the traditional close-to-close value that is standard and widely used as a proxy for realized volatility. Secondly, the extreme value estimator that uses daily low and high prices developed by Parkinson (1980) can be used. This method has the advantage that it does not require the constant volatility assumption mentioned earlier and according to Shu and Zhang (2003), the release of this restriction may result in a more accurate measurement of realized volatility. Thirdly, there is another range-based estimator that uses the daily high and low but also incorporates the opening jump into the pricing formula and therefore releases the continuous trading assumption included in other estimators. Due to the fact that opening jumps often occur when unexpected news was released during non-trading-days, the incorporation of these jumps may result in a better measurement of realized volatility. This method is also named after its developers, namely the Yang and Zhang (2000) volatility estimator. Finally, the fourth realized volatility estimator is computed from 5-minute intraday return data and is called "integrate volatility" by Andersen (2000). It is shown to improve the volatility estimation result significantly because high-frequency data contains more information for forecasting future volatility. Shu and Zhang (2003), conclude that the latter realized volatility estimator is the most predictable because it improves estimation by using high-frequency data.

4.5.3 Stochastic Volatility

As mentioned earlier, the BSM is based upon a number of assumptions that are to some degree counterfactual, such as constant volatility but there is the opportunity of relaxing this assumption by allowing volatility to vary randomly. As a consequence, the volatility smile curve can be accounted for by stochastic volatility models and the discrepancy between market-traded option prices and the Black-Scholes-predicted European option prices can be avoided. This procedure is meaningful in that much empirical research has shown that volatility definitely exhibits such random characteristics. Furthermore, fat-tailed return distributions can be simulated by stochastic volatility. To summarise, stochastic volatility models include powerful modifications to improve the description of a very complex market (Jean-Peirre, Papanicolaou and Sircar 2000). Well-known examples of stochastic volatility models are the Autoregressive Conditional Heteroscedasticity model

(ARCH) developed by Engle (1982) and the Generalized Autoregressive Conditional Heteroscedasticity model (GARCH). The latter is an extension of the Engle model allowing a more flexible lag structure and was introduced by Bollerslev (1986), but both are widely used models in recent studies to model stochastic volatility (Chen 1997). Since its introduction, the GARCH model has been extended in various ways like, for instance, the formulation of alternative volatility processes. The outcome is quite a large variety of GARCH models, such as the ARCH, GARCH, EGARCH, IGARCH, APARCH, or GJR, with different functional forms (Laurent and Peters 2002). There will be a comparison of some of these volatility models in the next chapter.

4.5.4 Comparison of Volatility Types

In general, there is a huge discrepancy across research results whether realized, implied or model volatility is best for forecasting future volatility. Nevertheless, the following paragraphs are aimed at providing a solid comparison of various studies discussing the predictive abilities of these volatility types, taking into account potential limitations included in this research.

In Poon and Granger (2003), they compared the research results of 93 studies about forecasting methods in order to find out which one provides the best volatility estimate. Therefore, they classified volatility forecasts as belonging in one of the following four categories. Firstly, HISVOL stands for historical volatilities and includes random walks, absolute returns, historical averages of squared returns, time series models using moving averages, exponential weights, etc. Second, GARCH includes all members of the ARCH, GARCH, EGARCH, etc. family. Third, ISD stands for option implied standard deviation, based on the BSM and various generalizations. And finally, the fourth category includes stochastic volatility models.

	Number of Studies	Studies Percentage
HISVOL > GARCH	22	56%
GARCH > HISVOL	17	44%
HISVOL > ISD	8	24%
ISD > HISVOL	26	76%
GARCH > ISD	1	6
ISD > GARCH	17	94
SV > HISVOL	3	
SV > GARCH	3	
GARCH > SV	1	
ISD > SV	1	

Figure 10: Pair-wise comparison of volatility forecasts

Figure 10 shows the pair-wise comparison of the results obtained by these studies. For those studies examining both, GARCH and HISVOL models, 22 studies or 56% found that HISVOL provides better volatility forecasts than GARCH models and 17 studies or 44% found that GARCH is better than HISVOL. One of those supporting the former theory is Figlewski (1997), who showed that by applying a simple projection of observed realized volatility into the future, a GARCH-type model can be outperformed. Moreover, realized volatility seems to perform better in predicting future volatility over longer forecast horizons than implied volatility, which will be explained later. On the other hand, Shu and Zhang (2003) argue that realized volatility has fewer explanatory abilities than IV because their results show that all the information contained in historical volatility has already been reflected by IV and consequently, realized volatility does not provide any incremental forecast ability. Moreover, the expectation that IV outperforms realized volatility is supported by the fact that options traders are mostly institutional traders and hence, have more information. If an implied volatility approach is chosen, the volatility smile phenomenon makes it unclear which IV provides the best predictor of volatility until option expiration. However, studies, including Poon and Granger (2003) and Beckers (1981), have shown that because of the low sensitivity to pricing errors and the high liquidity of at-the-money option, at-the-money IV outperforms any combination of available implied volatilities regarding forecasting ability. Ederington and Guan (2002), confirm this research finding, saying that after a bias correction, at-the-money IV can be a simple but good forecast of future volatility. As already mentioned earlier, the forecast ability can be improved by using high-frequency data of realized volatility from intraday 5-minutes returns Shu and Zhang (2003). According to Poon and Granger (2003), ISD is supposed to be the best forecasting method, followed by HISVOL and GARCH models which perform almost equally. Moreover the success of the implied volatility model is not surprising, because these forecasts are based on larger and more relevant information using option prices. In addition, seventeen of the 93 papers compared the GARCH model and its various versions. By comparing the results of these studies, it was found that GARCH dominates ARCH. On the one hand, models that include volatility asymmetry such as, for example, EGARCH or GJR-GARCH perform better than GARCH, but, on the other hand, certain specialized GARCH models such as FIGARCH or RSGARCH do better in certain studies.

These highly varying results support the fact that Granger and Poon do in fact also reflect on their research findings from a very critical perspective, because it seems to be obvious that every study is conducted in such a manner that it will support the viewpoint that one particular method is best. Moreover, some studies might not have been published if the required result had not been achieved and, it is an obvious weakness of such comparisons that each study is prepared for various reasons using different data samples, assets, time intervals between observations and different evaluation techniques. In addition, Ederington and Guan (2010) and Christoffersen and Diebold (2000) have observed that various studies on the evaluation of forecasting performance of different volatility models typically are focused on short time horizons but according to Poon and Granger (2003), there are more drawbacks that make research results difficult to interpret. Canina and Figlewski (1993) for instance, used overlapping data and in Christensen and Prabhala (1998), the heavily criticized Black-Scholes model was used for pricing American options. These studies are just examples to demonstrate that research results may vary depending on the methods applied and data selection. Blenman and Wang (2012) later extended the Christensen and Prabhala (1998) time horizon using multiple forecasting horizons in order to re-examine the relationship between implied and realized volatility. In the case of maturity intervals of one month, their research results are consistent with those of Christensen and Prabhala (1998), namely that at-the-money implied volatilities outperform past realized volatilities in terms of forecasting ability, but when the forecast horizon is extended to two months and also to three months, the forecasting ability of at-the-money IV decreases significantly relative to realized volatility. This tendency may be the result of a decreased efficiency of long-term option markets caused by low liquidity of longer-term options. Empirical research results obtained by Figlewski (1997) and Ederington and Guan (2006) confirm that the past realized volatility offers better volatility prediction over long-term forecast horizons. In other words, IV may be a better volatility forecast for short-term horizons but over longer time horizons, realized volatility may be preferred (Blenman and Wang 2012). It should be taken into consideration that there is also a critical discussion about the predictive ability of implied volatility included in chapter 6.3 about the VIX performance and critique.

In conclusion, financial market volatility can be caused by the release of new information and is influenced by the behaviour of humans reacting to the information release. Although volatility models are often based on assumptions that are not always correct, volatility is definitely forecastable using high-frequency data and the appropriate time horizon. To be more specific, implied volatility is a good forecast of future realized volatility, but for longer time horizons, historical volatility was found to perform better. Unfortunately, however, volatility predictability decays significantly and quickly as the corresponding time horizon increases, often as soon as 10 days. Finally, there seems to be a contradiction between theory and practice, as it can be observed with the BSM, which is heavily criticized in theory, but is still in wide-spread use in practice.

5 Behavioural Finance

As a further step, it is appropriate to examine the roots of financial market volatility and in doing so, analyse whether price movements can or cannot be explained by the rational behaviour of market participants or whether behavioural aspects influence financial volatility. Therefore, this chapter is organized as follows: first, the theoretical dimensions and historical dimensions of the EMH and behavioural finance are addressed briefly. Next, some critical opinions concerning the truthfulness of the EMH and arguments against the theory of efficient markets will be presented, always bearing in mind the influence of behavioural finance on financial market volatility.

5.1 Efficient Market Hypothesis and Behavioural Finance: A Description

During the 20th century, there was a wave of theorization that resulted amongst other things, in the Capital Asset Pricing Model (CAPM), arbitrage pricing and option pricing models. These approaches are highly normative and analytical and, assume a world dominated by "homo economicus", from a behavioural perspective (Olsen 1998). But as early as 1977, however, Roll (1977) already argued that the CAPM was probably unverifiable and in 1992, Eugene Fama, a key pioneer of the CAPM, withdrew his support from the model (Fama and French 1992). The story of the CAPM is a famous example that illustrates that many intentions to explain the structure and dynamics of asset prices ended in an imperfect solution. Over the last decades, the topic of behavioural finance enjoyed increasing recognition in the global financial markets and should provide solutions to some unanswered questions. In the following paragraphs, the concept of behavioural finance, the EMH and their differences are briefly explained.

Behavioural finance is the study of how psychological aspects impact financial decisions of individuals, markets and organizations (De Bondt et al. 2008). In Olsen (1998), the author defines behavioral finance similarly, but admits that even if behavioural finance does challenge various concepts and principles, it is not aimed at rejecting them totally if they are sound. Behavioral finance is based on the arguments of limited arbitrage and investor sentiment and offers an explanation for what some observers label excessive volatility (Olsen 1998, Lawrence, McCabe and Prakash 2007). All these aspects are discussed in more detail in the following sub-chapters. On the contrary, the EMH is based on three basic arguments, namely that investors are assumed to be rational and as they are, their trades are random and therefore, cancel each other out, having no effect on prices. In addition, if they are rational, they will be met by arbitrageurs who will eliminate any influence they have on the market (Lawrence et al. 2007). The arbitrage argument was already formulated by Fama (1965) and Friedman (1953), when they argued that due to arbitrage, security prices are brought in line with its intrinsic values, but over the last few decades, the EMH has been confronted with increasing criticism concerning its underlying assumptions and its concept of explaining the behaviour of financial market participants. The following chapter will cover some of these critical opinions.

5.2 Efficient Market Hypothesis: Critique

As already mentioned in the preceding chapter, the foundation of the EMH is based on the argument of the rational decision-making of investors. The rationality of investors was challenged, amongst others, by Black, who says that investors trade on noise rather than on information (Black 1986). Other researchers show that emotional crowds dominate market pricing and volatility and they drive prices based on the latest scenarios, whether they are optimistic or pessimistic. Although the events that trigger investors to respond emotionally are short-lived, the subsequent emotions are longer-lasting. On the other hand, the second argument on which the EMH builds its foundation is the assumption that arbitrageurs will move asset prices to their intrinsic value as soon as arbitrage opportunities arise (Howard 2013) but according to Howard (2013), who refers to research over the last 40 years in his article about behavioural portfolio management, arbitrage has not been able to eliminate price distortions and he gives three possible reasons for this: first, the difficulty of identifying arbitrage opportunities, the riskiness and costliness associated with arbitrage and finally, the limited number of market participants willing to engage in arbitrage. Recent results by (Cornell, Landsman and Stubben 2011) though, show that even if arbitrage opportunities are successfully identified, there is a tendency for market participants prefering to exacerbate sentiment-driven price movements, instead of dampening them as one would expect of rational behaviour. In other words, institutional professionals tend to join the emotional crowd rather than acting rationally and hence arbitrage appears to play a small role in stock picking. Besides, it is affirmed that more often prices and volatility measure emotions rather than underlying values and fundamentals, a consequence of arbitrage failing to keep prices in line with fundamentals (Howard 2013). Moreover, Grossman and Stiglitz (1980) argue that markets where security prices always equal their fundamental values provide no compensation for the cost of digging for information which might uncover deviations and therefore markets cannot be efficient.

Besides the foundations of the EMH, there are still other sources of criticism remaining that challenge its truthfulness. Shiller (1980), for instance, shows that stock prices move too much to be justified by Efficient Market Hypothesis as presented in Figure 11.

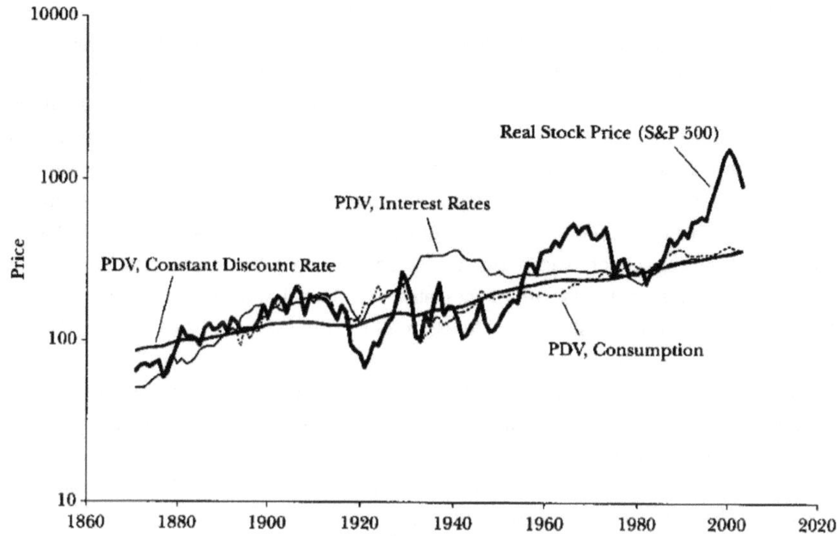

Figure 11: Real stock prices and present values of subsequent real dividends

By comparing the real stock price with the present value curve (present value subsequent to that year of the real dividends paid on the SPX, discounted by a constant real discount rate equal to the geometric average return between 1871-2002 on the SPX) it can be observed that the present value behaves remarkably like a stable trend, in contrast to the stock price. Consequently, Shiller argued that the stability of the present value over time suggests that there is excess volatility in the aggregate stock market.

According to Thaler (1999), traditional financial models based on the EMH are not able to explain anomalies in the markets such as high trading volume, abnormally high volatility and the formation and bursting of prices bubbles. The rise and bursting of bubbles can be better explained by behavioural finance, as can be seen in the following example: first, it is necessary to explain the term "sentiment" in this context. In behavioural finance literature, sentiment is defined as an individual's belief about the future performance of an asset. In this example, we consider that an investor with a low sentiment level makes trading at low prices possible. When they are eliminated after selling their shares, the stock price rises. As a consequence, different investor sentiment levels enable trading at various price ranges, causing stock prices to be more volatile. Investors' sentiment levels, however, may change over time depending on macroeconomic or firm-specific conditions, expert or analyst views and on false or insider information. This means that investors who sold stocks may purchase them again later at higher prices, which can lead to high trading volumes across every price level and can, therefore, result in stock prices above/below the fundamental price. When the number of low-sentiment investors is lower than the number of high-sentiment investors, demand will exceed supply, which is a potential catalyst for price escalation. If stock prices continue to rise, however, the number of high-sentiment traders will decrease and there will suddenly be more low-sentiment investors, a situation that is also called a regime shift. As a consequence, prices will decrease dramatically because the demand for high-sentiment investors has already been met and there are no buyers left to perceive a bargain. This situation can be compared with the bursting of a bubble (Lawrence et al. 2007). In general, the impact of sentiment on financial crises is more pronounced in countries which are culturally more sensitive to herd-behaviour and overreaction and countries with lower institutional development (Zouaoui et al. 2011, Rizzi 2008).

In conclusion, it can be summarized that business fundamentals alone do not explain the structure and dynamics of asset price movements and many arguments in favour of the EMH are simply not true, including rationality of market participants and unlimited arbitrage opportunities. However, behavioural finance offers a promising and plausible explanation for some of the previously mentioned phenomena that are difficult to explain explicitly with EMH, such as, for instance, excess volatility or the domination of emotions in asset pricing and financial decision-making.

6 VIX Index

As already mentioned in the introduction of this research paper, volatility forecasting is a wide-spread desire of financial professionals due to the various applications where volatility is a key input. Unfortunately, however, the process of volatility forecasting still sees itself confronted with an avalanche of critique, much of which is associated with weaknesses concerning the efficient market assumption. The following chapter has the purpose of clarifying whether the VIX Index provides a solution concerning these problems and explores the performance and predictive ability of the VIX. In doing so, this chapter initially starts with a section covering an introduction into the history of the VIX Index and the main reasons for its launch. Moreover, the calculation and some characteristics, such as the negative correlation between the VIX and the SPX, will be discussed. Next, is an overview of some strategies and opportunities to use the VIX for financial risk management objectives and, finally, there is a section presenting some critical opinions concerning the VIX.

6.1 An Introduction to the "Investor Fear Gauge"

The VIX Index is an index of the 30-day implied volatility implied by the prices of S&P 500 option contracts (CBOE 2014a). It was introduced in 1993 by the CBOE for purposes. First, it should provide a benchmark for expected short-term volatility and hence be a forward-looking index measuring the volatility that investors expect to see. Secondly, the VIX was intended to provide an index upon which options and futures contracts on volatility could be written. Figure 12 shows the development of the VIX Index over the last five years. In general, a high level of the VIX is related to a high level of fear among investors, whereas a low VIX level is associated with complacency (CBOE 2014c).

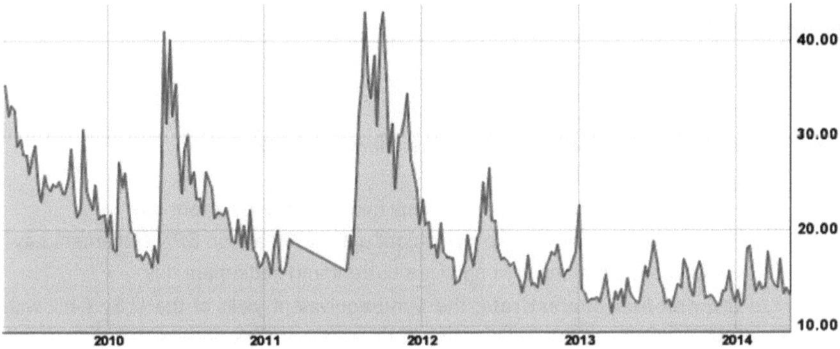

Figure 12: VIX chart over the last 5 years

The original index construction computes an average of the Black and Scholes option implied volatility with strike prices close to the current spot index level and maturities interpolated at about one month (Carr and Wu 2004). According to Whaley (2008), any implied volatility index must be based on prices from a deep and active index option market, such as the Standard & Poor's 100 Index (OEX). In 1992, OEX options accounted for 75% of the total index option volume and were hence the most actively traded index options in the United States. Additionally, the VIX Index was based on the prices of eight options, which were the most actively traded of the option series available at that time, but over the years, the structure of index option trading has changed in two fundamental ways in the U.S. Firstly, the SPX option market became the most active index option market, with SPX options traded over 12 times as frequently as OEX options and secondly, the trading motives of investors in the index option market changed. Concerning the latter, the role of index put and call options changed from an equally important role to an imbalanced role. Due to an increasing domination of portfolio insurers who regularly buy out-of-the-money and at-the-money index puts for insurance purposes, the volume of SPX puts was 72% higher than the volume of SPX calls (Whaley 2008). Secondly, the original computation methodology has drawn criticism from both industry and academia for its upward bias induced by the trading-day conversion. Consequently, the CBOE changed the VIX Index computation in 2003 to account for these developments and weaknesses. They not only began to use SPX instead of OEX option prices, but they also included out-of-the-money options and finally, the upward bias induced in the original calculation was eliminated by annualizing following the actual/365 day-counting convention (Carr and Wu 2004). Ever since, the formula used in the VIX calculation has been:

$$\sigma^2 = \frac{2}{T}\sum_i \frac{\Delta K_i}{K_i^2} e^{RT} Q(K_i) - \frac{1}{T}\left[\frac{F}{K_0} - 1\right]^2$$

Equation 2: VIX formula

where...

- **T is the time to expiration** given by the following expression:
  T = (Exchange) / Minutes in a year
  - $M_{\text{Current day}}$: Minutes remaining until midnight of the current day
  - $M_{\text{Settlement day}}$: Minutes from midnight until 08:30 am on SPX settlement day
  - $M_{\text{other days}}$: Total minutes between current and settlement day
- **R is the risk-free interest rate**, the bond-equivalent yield of the U.S. T-bill with the closest maturity to the expiry dates of the relevant SPX options.

- **F is the forward index level** derived from index option prices by the following expression:
  - F = Strike Price / e^{RT} x (Call Prices – Put Price)
- **K_0 is the first strike below the forward index level F**
- **K_i is the strike price of the i-th (out-of-the-money) option:**
  - Call if $K_i > K_0$
  - Put if $K_i < K_0$
  - Both put and call if K_i equals K_0
- **ΔK_i is the interval between strike prices** calculated as:
  - $\Delta K_i = (K_{t+1} - K_{t+1}) / 2$
  - At the lowest strike price it is simply the difference between the lowest and the next higher strike and for the highest strike it is the difference between the highest and the next lower strike.
- **$Q(K_i)$ is the midpoint of the bid-ask spread for each option with strike K_i** (Exchange 2009).

This formula results in a gradually declining weighting per strike, depending on how far out-of-the-money the options are which is shown in Figure 13 (Wintner 2013).

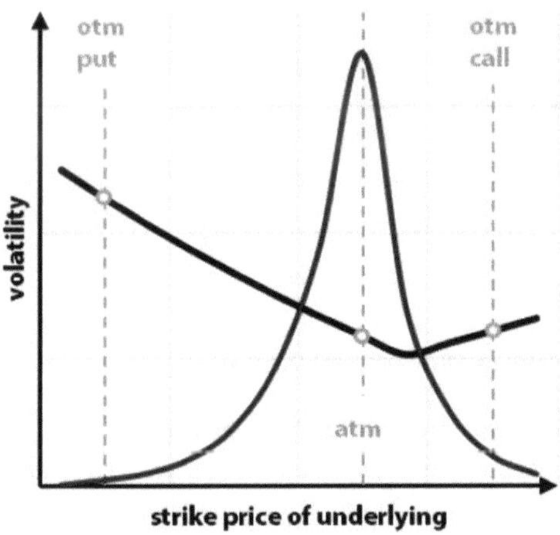

Figure 13: Weighting scheme of the VIX Index calculation

However, the CBOE is confronted with some criticism concerning their procedure for calculating the VIX level. Chapter 6.3 provides further information in this regard.

Since its introduction, the "investor fear gauge", as the VIX is also called, is a widely used indicator of investor greed and fear towards the market (Whaley 2008). On the one hand, factors that will cause greed include over optimism, overconfidence caused by an underestimation of risks, excessive levels of longing, etc. On the other hand, fear is referred to an uncertain feeling towards situational control and people with fear will make pessimistic judgments of future events (Li and Wang 2013). Whereas a prolonged and/or extremely high VIX level indicates a high degree of anxiety in the market, a prolonged and/or extremely low index level is a sign of a high degree of complacency. Consequently, the first situation is regarded as a bullish indicator and the latter one as a bearish indicator (Cipollini and Manzini 2007). The traditional explanation for this inverse relationship between the SPX and the VIX Index is that as soon as the market declines and shows signs of weakness, investors panic and rush to buy index puts, which creates an imbalance in the supply and demand equilibrium. The consequence is a rise in option prices relative to the market level and thereby an increase in implied volatility (Bittman 2007). Figure 14 shows the development of the negative correlation between the SPX and the VIX between 2004 and 2012.

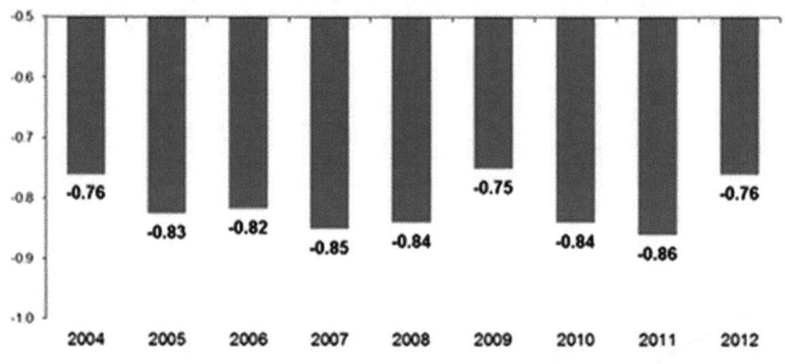

Figure 14: Negative correlations of daily returns of S&P 500 and VIX Index

Although the correlation between the two indexes varies between -0.75 in 2009 and -0.86 in 2011, the correlation can be interpreted as being stable and highly negative (CBOE 2014b). Furthermore, Figure 15 shows the inverse relationship between the indexes since 1990 (Dshort.com 2014).

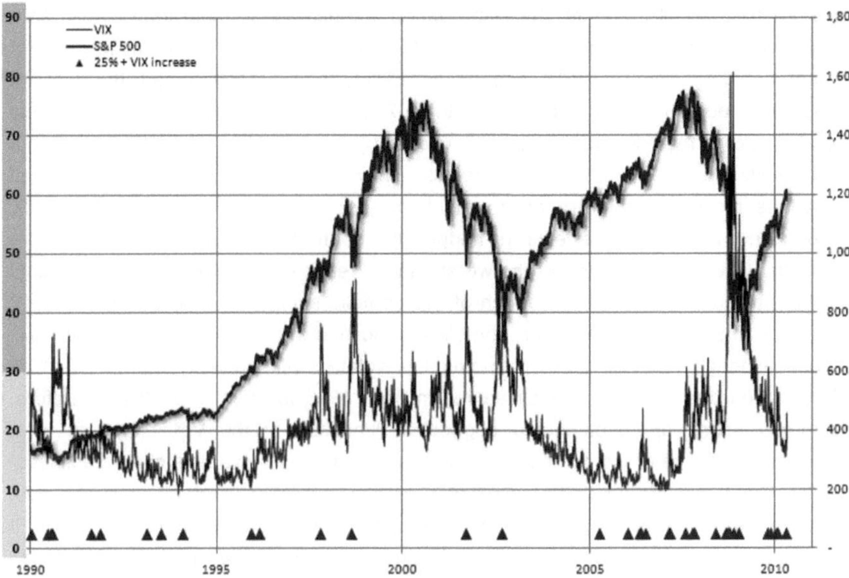

Figure 15: Inverse relationship between the SPX & VIX Index

As a consequence, this suggests that a portfolio combination of the SPX and the VIX Index should provide diversification benefits but this aspect will be discussed in the next chapter. The correlation analysis between the SPX and the VIX will be the introductory analysis of the empirical part of this research paper. See chapter 7.1 for further information.

6.2 Applications and Strategies

Due to the high negative correlation between the SPX and the VIX, a portfolio combination of these indexes should provide diversification benefits, because large negative correlation combined with the appropriate weights can provide risk-reducing benefits with a minimal reduction in returns. Daigler and Rossi (2006) found that the combination of the SPX and the VIX reduces portfolio risk and the overall benefits of including volatility as an asset seem to be significant. The following example illustrates the advantages that may arise by including the VIX in an investment portfolio: consider a portfolio worth $100,000 of which 90% are invested in the S&P 500 and the remaining 10% are invested in the VIX. During the investment period between July 7 and September 28 in 1998, the SPX fell from 1184 to 956, a decline of 19% resulting in a portfolio loss of $17,000. The VIX on the contrary, rose from 16.23 to 44.28 during the same period, an increase of more than 250%. As a consequence, if the trader had invested directly in the VIX Index, the portfolio gains of $25,000 resulting from the VIX rise would clearly have outperformed the loss of $17,000 incurred by the SPX decrease (Bittman 2007). However, the inverse relationship does also applies to hedge funds, as was explored by Dash and Moran (2005) for different return environments. Their research results show that there is an asymmetry of correlations for different return environments of hedge funds. In particular, the VIX may provide diversification benefits for hedge fund portfolios when they deliver negative returns and when the funds deliver the worst quartile returns. But the question that should be asked in return would be how much of the portfolio should one allocate to the VIX? In general, there are no efficient portfolios allocating more than 10% to the VIX, because although the VIX return distribution is volatile, with monthly returns +/- 10% fairly common, the average annualized return from 1995 to 2004 is 0.07%. Therefore, a common sense approach would suggest a limitation of the VIX exposure to a small amount. By referring to the already mentioned mean-reverting characteristic of volatility, Dash and Moran (2005) devised a tactical allocation strategy. If in the past quarter the VIX increased by over 20%, VIX allocation is cut down to 0% and if it decreased by more than 20%, then the VIX exposure is increased to 10%. If changes are between +/- 20%, the portfolio exposure of the VIX is kept steady at 5%.

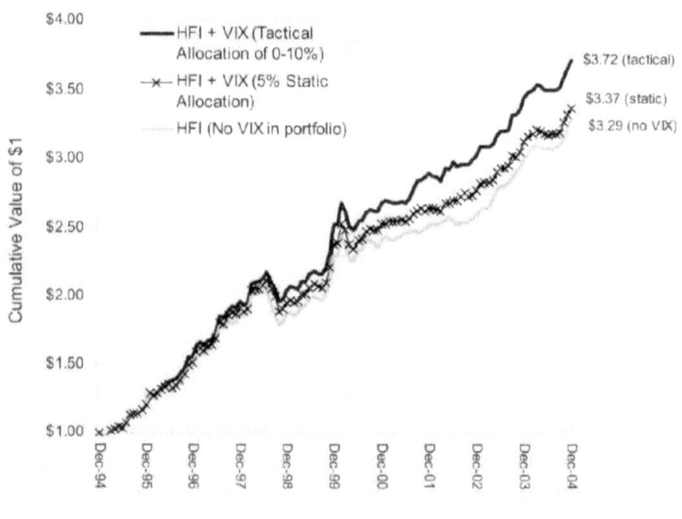

Figure 16: Cumulative returns of HFI and VIX portfolio

Figure 16 shows the cumulative return of three $1 portfolios (VIX and CSFB/Tremont hedge Fund Index – HFI) between 1994 and 2004, namely one portfolio with a tactical VIX allocation between 0 and 10%, one with a static allocation of 5% and finally, a portfolio without VIX exposure. As you can see, the tactical VIX allocation portfolio continuously outperforms the other portfolios over the whole investment period and a static exposure results in better returns than the portfolio in which the VIX is totally abandoned (Dash and Moran 2005). However, due to the fact that it is not possible to invest directly in the VIX itself, VIX future and options, whose payoffs depend on the future VIX values, were created in order to provide the opportunity to invest in volatility and reduce volatility risk (Deng, McCann and Wang 2012). It has been possible to trade VIX options and futures on the Chicago Futures Exchange (CFE), which is part of the CBOE, since March 2004 (Daigler and Rossi 2006). VIX futures can provide an effective opportunity to diversify portfolios, hedge equity returns and to spread implied volatility against realized volatility (Bittman 2007). However, VIX futures are different from the traditional contracts because there is no underlying cash commodity. As a consequence, there is no arbitrage-pricing relation and hence no opportunities for arbitrageurs. This means that the VIX can rise/fall dramatically but the price of the futures contract will not necessarily move with the same intensity. To be precise, the price of VIX futures contracts represents the market's expectation of the 30-day implied volatility of S&P 500 options at expiry date.

In addition, a position in volatility can also be established by using over-the-counter instruments, such as variance swaps or forward variance swaps (Daigler and Rossi 2006). Variance swaps settle to backward-looking volatility realizations, because their payoff is a linear function of the difference between realized and agreed variance at strike date. VIX futures and variance swaps on the contrary, settle at quantities that reflect expectations concerning future volatility and to the price at which volatility exposure can be bought in the future. Besides, another distinction between VIX futures and variance swaps is that whereas the latter ones are based around variance and hence, its payoffs are more volatile, VIX futures are based around standard deviation. In general, the payoff of volatility products depends on two aspects, namely any unexpected changes in volatility over the term of the contract and on any risk premiums impounded into the price. Due to the fact that expectations regarding future volatility are already incorporated in the pricing, only unexpected changes should matter for payoffs. On the one hand, shorting volatility in specific one-month variance swaps, offers the opportunity of capturing substantial risk premi ums. The disadvantage of this strategy can be an increasing risk that the downside is exacerbated during market declines, especially when the investment portfolio contains substantial equity exposure. This strategy is particularly attractive for investors with longer investment horizons, a secure basis of funding, lower risk aversion and with portfolios that are less dominated by equities. Long positions in longer-dated VIX futures or forward variance swaps, on the other hand, offer the possibility of hedging equity risk at little cost and contain minimal exposure to the volatility risk premium (Warren 2012). Unfortunately, VIX derivatives are not able to satiate investors' demand for volatility investments, due to institution-intern restrictions. Moreover, many retail customers are simply too small to participate in the derivative market (Whaley 2013). As a consequence, exchange-traded products (ETPs) linked to futures contracts on the VIX were launched in 2009 and have been heavily traded ever since. ETPs are securities that are designed to provide price exposure that investors find difficult to obtain on their own and are defined by an easily identifiable benchmark, such as the SPX or crude oil. Considering the fact that these instruments incur losses on a frequent basis, one might ask the question: why are they still traded as much. Unfortunately, it seems that many traders who invest in ETPs think that they are investing in the VIX itself, but as we already know, the VIX is not a traded security. This argument and the fact the ETPs are certain to lose money through time suggest that a significant number of traders are irrational and/or unaware of how ETPs are structured and perform over time (Whaley 2013).

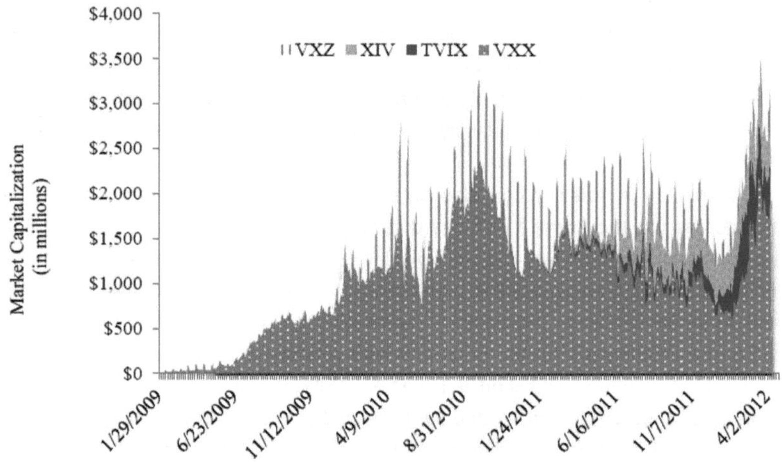

Figure 17: Market capitalization of the four largest VIX futures ETPs

During the last few years, the number of ETPs, the market capitalization and trading volume has increased enormously (Deng et al. 2012). In particular, more than 30 VIX-ETPs were listed in 2013 with an aggregate market capitalization of 4 billion dollars and a daily trading volume of 800 million dollars. The enormous growth of these products, which is shown in Figure 17, is amazing because the long-term expected value of ETPs is zero and since its introduction, ETPs linked to SPX/VIX futures short-term indices have incurred losses of over $4 billion. Even in the absence of transaction fees, these products are destined to result in losses. Even more surprisingly is that the market still continues to grow (Whaley 2013).

After providing information about the main strategies of implementing volatility in investment portfolios, there will be a discussion about critical opinions with regards to the VIX Index and associated instruments.

6.3 Critical Evaluation and Predictive Performance of the VIX

In 2010, the Seattle Times published a newspaper article in which they referred to a study by Laszlo Birinyi and analyst Kevin Pleines who analysed the predictive performance of the VIX Index. They heavily criticize the VIX Index and its performance as a volatility forecast, which is illustrated by the following quotes:

> *"The VIX is a coincidental indicator with limited predictive value".*
>
> *"It details, perhaps better than other measures, the volatility of the market today, but not tomorrow or the day after."*

Furthermore, they argue that the VIX Index is all but useless for forecasting the future direction of equity prices. Instead, Birinyi and Pleines claim that the VIX Index moves in lock-step with stock prices (Kisling 2010).

What are the main weaknesses of the VIX Index that result in criticism? The following subchapters provide a brief overview of the main assumptions and weaknesses of the VIX Index and its computation that cause criticism.

6.3.1 Implied Volatility and the Assumption of Constant Volatility

As already mentioned in chapter 6.1, the VIX Index is based on implied volatility, which assumes volatility to be constant, but by now it is fairly well established both in theory and practice that this is definitely not the case. In particular, studies such as Ferris, Kim and Park (2010), and Bakshi and Kapadia (2003), have proven the opposite. Both research studies followed the same procedure, namely calculating the gains to a delta hedged strategy. The theory behind this procedure is the following that if volatility is constant, then there is no risk premium for volatility changes and hence gains to a delta hedged strategy should be zero. If volatility is not constant, then volatility is priced in the market and you should expect to see negative gains to such a strategy, since options provide hedging due to the negative correlation between volatility and the underlying price level. The results of both studies are consistent and show that the gains to such a strategy yield negative returns indicating non-constant volatility.

In consideration of the discussion concerning constant volatility, there is still a lot of research being conducted to analyse the information quality of implied volatility. In general, there is a huge amount of discrepancies in research results with regards to the predictive ability of implied volatility. Whereas Ferris et al. (2010) report that they find strong support for the efficiency and unbiasedness of implied volatility as an estimator for realized future volatility, Jorion (1995), Jackwerth and Rubinstein (1996), Fleming (1998), Ederington and Guan (2002) and Bakshi and Kapadia (2003) conclude that implied volatility is, compared to historical and realized future volatility, almost always upward biased and, consequently, they interpret their findings as inconsistent with the constant volatility assumption, but despite the non-constant inconsistency, options traders still rely on implied volatilities derived from BSM when making trading decisions. Traders believe that fundamental price information is included in these implied volatility measures. In other words, there is a huge contradiction between research findings and the application of practitioners.

6.3.2 Asymmetry of Daily Changes

Moreover, there are researchers that are convinced that weaknesses regarding the computation lead to under-/overestimation of the true volatility. Due to the demand for portfolio insurance, the relation between the changes in the SPX and the VIX is asymmetric, as can be observed by the following example. In the case of an SPX rise of 100 basis points (bps), the VIX will fall by -2.99% and if the SPX falls by 100 bps, then the VIX will rise by 4.5 percentage points. In other words, the VIX is more a barometer of traders' fear of a market downturn than a barometer of investors' excitement in a market upturn (Whaley 2009). Moreover, Jiang and Tian (2007), found that the new VIX computation method requires several approximations and some of them may produce substantial errors. Consequently, they propose a modified calculation method applying a smoothing algorithm which is presented at a later stage of this chapter. Nwogugu (2012) presents in his article many calculation errors that lead to an inaccurate and inefficient index whose calculation is wrong and misleading. As mentioned earlier, the VIX formula for calculating the VIX is as follows:

$$\sigma^2 = \frac{2}{T}\sum_i \frac{\Delta K_i}{K_i^2} e^{RT} Q(K_i) - \frac{1}{T}\left[\frac{F}{K_0} - 1\right]^2 \tag{1}$$

Firstly, Wagner, Ellis and Dubofsky (1996) and Ahn, Byoun and Park (2003) already showed that the put-call parity is often violated even after accounting for transaction costs and thus the derived forward options price ("F" in the VIX formula) is wrong (Bharadwaj and Wiggins 2001). Secondly, F/K_0 does not reflect the true magnitude of market direction and profitability of the option, not only because F is wrong, but also because K_0 may not be the nearest strike price at which the values of the call and put are closest. A more accurate definition of K_0 would be the strike price that is closest to the current price of the index. Third, $(F/K_0 - 1)^2$ converts negative returns into positive numbers so that the variance/volatility measure cannot express directional trends. Furthermore, this term implies that stocks that have many in-the-money options are less volatile than stocks with fewer in-the-money options. Fourth, T is already computed as a percentage of the total of amount of minutes each year, and consequently (1/T) is redundant. Fifth, only out-of-the-money options are used when deriving implied volatility, whereas in-the-money options also contain important information. Moreover, the term $(\Delta K_i/K_i^2)*e^{(rt)}$ implies that stocks with higher price ranges always have lower volatility compared to shares in lower price ranges through squaring the strike prices. In addition, the VIX is not accurate because the contribution of single options to the VIX does not depend on whether it is a put or call option, which are treated the same way over all strike prices. This distinction, however, is critical for determining implied volatility, because research has shown that implied volatilities of put and call options is not only different, but also that IV changes depending on how far the option (put or call) is in-the-money or out-of-the money. For instance, for strike prices that are far out-of-the money, puts may have higher IV than calls and for strike prices that are near-the-money, the situation is completely reversed (Nwogugu 2012).

Jiang and Tian (2007), also find that although the new VIX concept is more appealing than its predecessor, it may still underestimate the true volatility by as much as 198 index bps or overestimate it by 79 bps. Due to the fact that each bp is worth 10 dollars per VIX futures contract, these discrepancies are significant. Furthermore, these errors exhibit predictable patterns depending on volatility levels. As already mentioned, Jiang and Tian (2007) propose a simple smoothing method for extracting the model-free implied variance that is based on the construction of the IV function using an interpolation-extrapolation technique. The VIX Index calculated using this method is consistently accurate for all volatility and index levels. In general, the errors are within 5 bps and the maximum error is 8 bps, whereas the CBOE procedure results in errors from +79 to -198 bps.

6.3.3 The VIX Index vs. the CSFB Index

Another opportunity to assess the performance of the VIX Index is to compare it with a similar indicator, namely the Credit Suisse Fear Barometer (hereinafter CSFB). The CSFB uses longer-dated options (3 months) and is designed to price opportunity costs of buying downside protection. This protection is achieved by selling a 10% out-of-the-money call on the SPX and using the premium to purchase protection. In general, the higher the CSFB level, the more expensive is the protection resulting in a higher level of fear in the market.
Figure 18 shows the development of the CSFB and the VIX Index between March 2011 and 2012. Although they are both designed to measure similar issues, they sometimes

seem to diverge enormously which is highlighted by the arrows between January and March 2012 when the CSFB climbed and the VIX declined in contrast. However, there are many time intervals for which the two indexes seem to correlate negatively. The logical

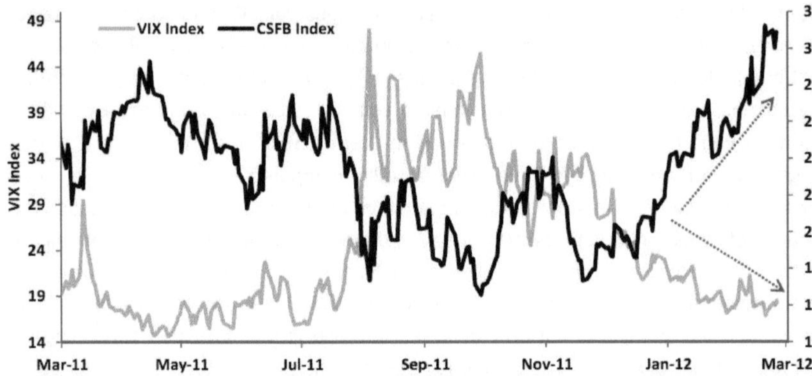

Figure 18: CSFB vs. VIX - Is fear high or low?

question that comes up when interpreting Figure 18 is whether the CSFB outperforms the VIX or vice-versa. Figure 19 indicates that the VIX is not always able to anticipate major

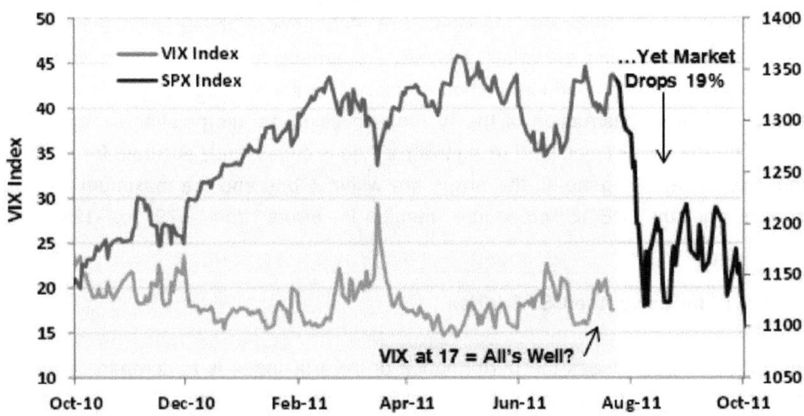

Figure 19: VIX and anticipation of major market corrections

market corrections as happened in August 2011, when the SPX dropped by 19% within days. During the weeks before the market downturn, the VIX was trading steadily at a range between 15 and 20, indicating that everything was fine.

Table 4 shows five examples when the VIX failed to predict major market sell-offs during the last twelve years by comparing the level of SPX decline with the level of the VIX one week before.

Crisis	VIX Level 1-Week Prior	Subsequent SPX Decline
Recession Mar'02	19	-34%
Subprime Oct'07	17	-19%
Lehman Sep'08	20	-50%
Greece May'10	19	-15%
Debt Ceiling Aug'11	19	-19%

Table 4: VIX level before major SPX declines

Figure 20 shows the CSFB plotted against the SPX between July 2007 and December 2011. Compared to the historical level, the CSFB was rather high in August 2011 when the VIX failed to anticipate the market correction. Furthermore, there are three examples that show that the CSFB performs reasonably well in indicating

Figure 20: The CSFB and the S&P 500 Index

market shifts which are pointed out by the pairs of cycles. First, the CSFB experienced a high of 29 (which is a signal for a high level of fear) in May 2007 just two months before the subprime mortgage crisis started. Second, another example of market downturn anticipation took place in April 2011 when the CSFB reached its all-time high of 30. Three months later there was an enormous sell-off, but the CSFB did not only anticipate market downturns, but also market rallies. In October 2008, the index reached an extreme low four months before the SPX bottomed out. In conclusion, the CSFB has frequently been able to anticipate major changes in investor sentiment.

6.3.4 Performance of a Probabilistic Interpretation

Next, the performance of the VIX Index as a predictor of future volatility will be assessed. In general, the VIX has a simple probabilistic interpretation concerning the expected range of the rate of return on the SPX level over the next 30 days. In order to apply this

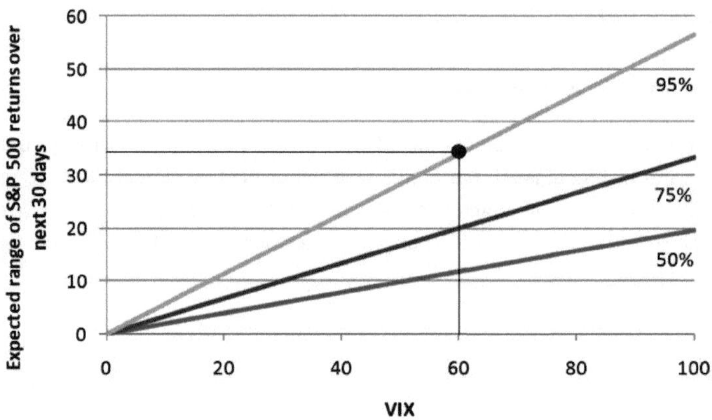

Figure 21: Expected range of SPX returns conditional on current VIX level

interpretation, Figure 21 can be used as follows. We assume that the current VIX level is 60 and consequently, the chance that the SPX will rise/fall by less than 34% over the next 30 days is 95%. This situation is shown by the black point. Following the same procedure, there is a 50/50 chance that the SPX will rise/fall by less than or more than 11.5% and a 75% chance that it will rise or fall by less than 20% over the next 30 days. The obvious question is how well this rule performs in practice and therefore, Whaley performed a simple test. Using a sample period of 274 months, he recorded the VIX level at the beginning of each month and based on this level, the expected range of return was computed. Of the 274 observations, 34.7% fell outside the 50% range, 7.3% fell outside the 75% range and only 1.1% fell outside the 95 percentage points range. In other words, the VIX Index performs rather well in predicting the magnitude of the SPX movement (Whaley 2009). Please note that this probabilistic interpretation only provides hints concerning the magnitude of the future move of the SPX, but it does not provide information regarding the direction of the SPX movement. Cipollini and Manzini (2007), come to the same conclusion, but also provide information with regards to the direction. They say that there is a meaningful relation between the three-month forward SPX future log-returns and the VIX Index.

Specifically, the SPX returns are expected to be high for a higher level or even spikes of implied volatility and vice-versa, future returns are supposed to be lower for low implied volatility levels. These results provide support for the hypothesis that a high level of implied volatility is a clear signal for an attractive entry point for long positions (Cipollini and Manzini 2007). Giot (2005) agrees that positive returns can be expected for long positions triggered by extremely high levels of implied volatility indexes. After investigating the predictive ability of the VIX Index on a daily basis for a period of seven years from 1986 to 1992, Fleming, Ostdiek and Whaley (1995) conclude that the VIX works well as a predictor for future realized stock market volatility. Becker, Clements and McClelland (2009), tested whether the VIX subsumes information regarding the contribution of historical jump activity to price volatility and also examined whether the VIX provides additional information concerning future jumps. Their data sample consists of over 3,400 observations from 1990 until 2003 and it was found that the VIX does indeed subsume information on historical jump activities. In other words, option markets do not react only to volatility resulting from continuous pricing processes when forming their forecasts, but also to discontinuous price jumps. However, it is interesting that the option market seems to need jump activities over a number of days to believe that this is not an occasional shock and then revise their forecasts (Becker et al. 2009).

6.3.5 VIX Manipulation

The following example shows that sometimes the VIX level is clearly manipulated. On March 13th, 2012 the VIX "whipsawed" sharply, moving back and forth between 14.9 and 16.0 three times within a duration of two hours. The SPX, on the other hand, rose monotonically over the same period, which is illustrated in Figure 22 and Figure 23. This is quite

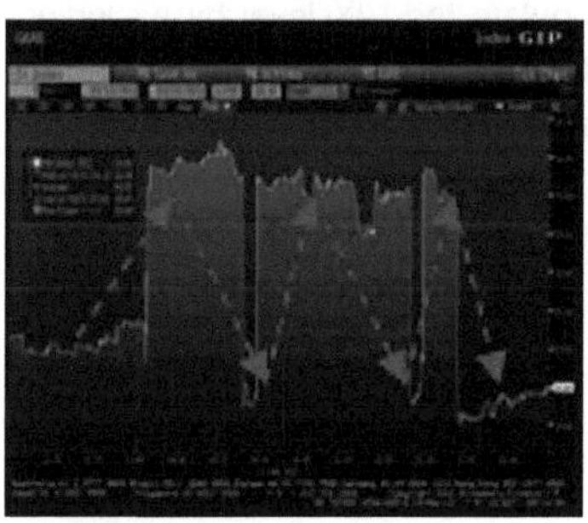

Figure 22: VIX „whipsaws"

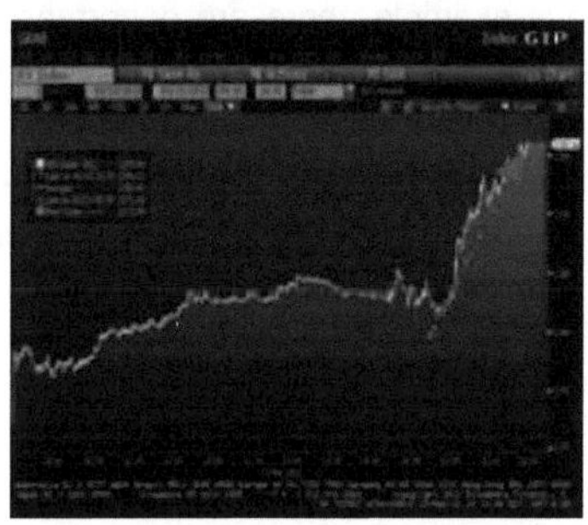

Figure 23: SPX advance over the same period

surprising as it would be expected that the VIX falls gradually as the SPX rose due to the negative correlation. This can be explained by the fact that in practice only a small fraction of the continuum of SPX strikes located round the at-the-money strike is actually liquid and observable. Due to the illiquidity of the far out-of-the-money option strikes, small changes in options premiums for these strikes can in practice disproportionally affect the VIX calculation. In order to insulate the VIX from these illiquid data points, the VIX methodology excludes all SPX option strikes from the calculation as soon as two consecutive "zero" bids are met (Tom 2012). Very often, this rule is rather a good tool to identify the point of illiquidity across the SPX put strikes. On this particular day, however, April SPX put strikes were bid from the at-the-money strikes down to the 800 strike, with the exception of the April 1045 and the April 1040 put strikes. When these bids were nulled, the volatility contribution accorded by SPX strikes from 800 to 1040 were snapped off from calculation, resulting in a VIX that decreased by more than one VIX point. Similarly, as soon as a bid is encountered for one of these strikes, it is then calculated using the full range starting from SPX strike 800, causing the VIX to increase again.

In conclusion, it was shown in this chapter that including volatility as an asset in portfolios in order to achieve diversification benefits very much pays off due to the high negative correlation between the VIX and the SPX Index. To be exact, high levels of implied volatility are good signs for an attractive entry spot. Nevertheless, the literature review demonstrated that although some studies argue that the VIX is definitely a good predictor of future volatility, there are also many weaknesses regarding its computation and assumptions, for instance. Moreover, the VIX is supposed to be an asymmetric barometer that overemphasizes economic downturns and underestimates periods of economic growth. Furthermore, it was illustrated that the VIX is often not able to anticipate major market declines as was done by the CSFB, but it is always essential to differentiate whether market sell-offs were based on unpredictable and unlikely events such as bankruptcies or whether certain market developments were obviously foreseeable. As it was illustrated by the previous example, there are opportunities to manipulate the VIX level by excluding specific strikes from computation. Finally, although ETPs are expected to generate high levels of losses, the enormous growth rates in this market indicate that investors are not perfectly informed and hence cannot decide rationally. As a consequence, this market growth is an obvious argument against the efficient market hypothesis.

7 Empirical Results

In the following subchapters there will be a presentation of the obtained research findings. In the quantitative part, the causal relationship between the S&P 500 Index and the VIX Index and their forecastability was analysed, whereas the qualitative analysis focused on the discussion of the obtained findings from the literature review and the Granger causality test by interviewing industry experts. In chapter 8, there will be a discussion of the empirical results presented here with respect to the existing literature, resulting in the answers to the research questions and hypotheses.

7.1 Quantitative Research

As was already mentioned in the methodological description, a Granger causality test was conducted in order to examine the causal relationship between the SPX and the VIX Index. In the following paragraphs, the obtained findings will be presented, starting with the descriptive analysis that consists of the correlation analysis and the normal distribution assessment, leading to the results of the Granger causality test. For a brief summary of the quantitative research findings, skip to Figure 33.

7.1.1 Descriptive Analysis

Correlation between SPX and VIX

	2003-2006	2007-2008	2009-2013
Pearson Correlation	-0,704	-0,765	-0,772
Sig. (2-tailed)	0,000	0,000	0,000

Table 5: Correlation between SPX and VIX Index for each period (untransformed)

Table 5 shows the Pearson correlation for each time period. In general, it can be observed that since 2003, the correlation between the SPX and the VIX Index varied between -0.704 and -0.772 and seems to approximate the value of -1. As was already mentioned in chapter 6.1, the inverse relationship between the two indexes is relatively stable over time.

Over the whole observation period, which amounts to 2,766 log-returns, the Pearson correlation score is -0.746, as it can be seen in Figure 24. Furthermore, the p-value is smaller than the defined confidence interval of 5% and, consequently, the correlation between the SPX and the VIX Index of -0.746 from 2003 until 2013 is statistically significant. Figure 25

Correlations

		SPX (2003-2013)	VIX (2003-2013)
SPX (2003-2013)	Pearson Correlation	1	-,746**
	Sig. (2-tailed)		,000
	N	2766	2766
VIX (2003-2013)	Pearson Correlation	-,746**	1
	Sig. (2-tailed)	,000	
	N	2766	2766

**. Correlation is significant at the 0.01 level (2-tailed).

Figure 24: Pearson Correlation between SPX & VIX 2003-2013 (untransformed)

illustrates the inverse relationship by comparing the daily log returns of the SPX and the VIX between 2003 and 2013. The monotonically decreasing regression line indicates the highly negative correlation between the two indexes. In general, it can be observed that there are not many outliers over the whole scatterplot. In the second step of the

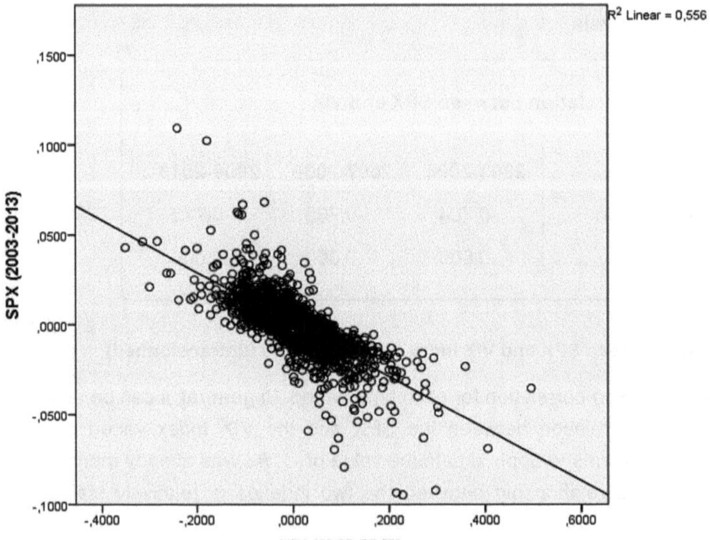

Figure 25: Correlation between SPX & VIX Index (untransformed)

descriptive analysis, the data of each time period was analysed regarding its normality of distribution in order to assess whether the data is skewed and/or includes kurtosis. Figure 26 shows the skewness and kurtosis for each time period, including an additional data set in which all observations between 2003 and 2013 were analysed. The data shows that the skewness and kurtosis are quite similar across all periods. As a result, particularly the normality plots and SPSS tables of the SPX between 2003 and 2006 are presented in this chapter, but all the other figures are included in the Appendix. By applying the criterion for normal distribution presented in Table 2 it is observable that the skewness level of the SPX tends to be slightly negative, but remains close to zero, whereas the skew of the VIX is positive and moves closer to the critical value of 1,000 each period.

Regarding the second test method, it was found that only in three time periods (SPX 2003-2006 and 2007-2008, VIX 2009-2013) the doubling of the standard error term resulted in a value higher than the skewness level. These interpretations lead to the conclusion that in some time periods the data is slightly skewed and as a consequence, the data series have to be transformed. Furthermore, it was found that the log-returns of the SPX and the VIX Index are highly leptokurtic, with kurtosis values ranging from 1,405 to 7,211, whereat the SPX tends to be more leptokurtic. Therefore, when choosing the appropriate Lambda value for the Box-Cox transformation, the aim was not only to choose a parameter that would result in better skewness level as a first priority, but also to reduce kurtosis.

Descriptive Statistics

	N	Skewness		Kurtosis	
	Statistic	Statistic	Std. Error	Statistic	Std. Error
SPX (2003-2006)	1006	,020	,077	1,405	,154
VIX (2003-2006)	1006	,333	,077	3,203	,154
SPX (2007-2008)	503	-,187	,109	7,211	,217
VIX (2007-2008)	503	,667	,109	3,893	,217
SPX (2009-2013)	1257	-,276	,069	4,161	,138
VIX (2009-2013)	1257	,730	,069	3,920	,138
SPX (2003-2013)	2766	-,320	,047	10,783	,093
VIX (2003-2013)	2766	,687	,047	4,618	,093
Valid N (listwise)	503				

Figure 26: Skewness and kurtosis for each period (untransformed)

Figure 27 shows the normality plot of the untransformed SPX log-returns between 2003 and 2006. As is clearly observable, the data series is characterized by a high degree of kurtosis, but after the data transformation mentioned in 2.3 (with a Lambda of 1,8 for the SPX in this period) the time series is way more normally distributed.

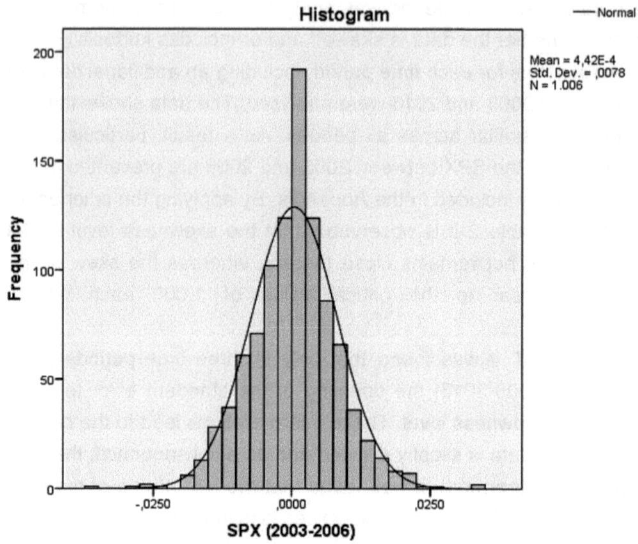

Figure 27: Normality plot SPX 2003-2006 (untransformed)

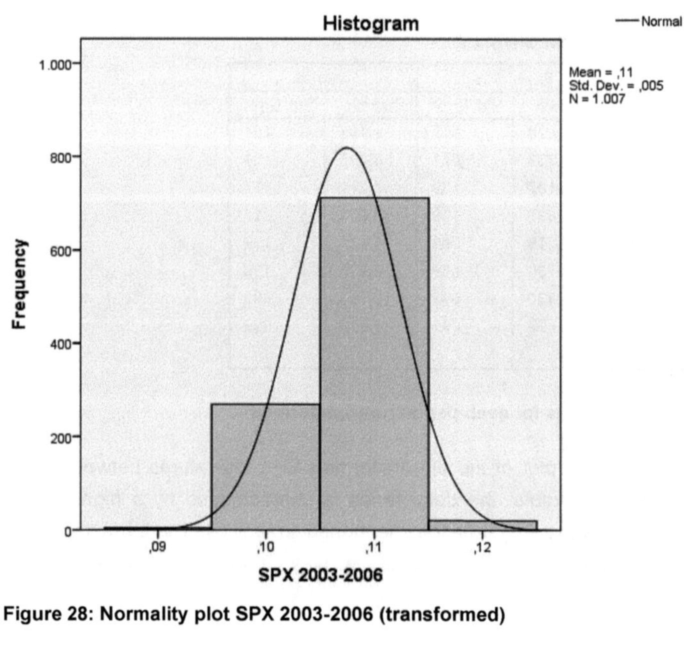

Figure 28: Normality plot SPX 2003-2006 (transformed)

By taking a look at Figure 28 it can be seen that the leptokurtic characteristic has diminished. Furthermore, it is notable that the data set is now more similar to a normal distribution curve. The same procedure was applied for each time period and for both indexes, and the results obtained are presented in the appendix of this research paper, including all SPSS plots and tables. Nevertheless, it must be mentioned that for the Granger causality test, the untransformed data set was entered into the software. This was necessary because the Box-Cox transformation parameters were explicitly computed in order to find the most appropriate Lambdas that would later be entered into the software. The transformation within the Granger causality test itself was performed by the "Bivariate Granger Causality – Free Statistics Software". In the following chapter the causal relationship between the SPX and the VIX Index is discussed.

7.1.2 Granger Causality Test

The following figures show the p-values for the Granger causality between the SPX and the VIX for each period in order to assess whether the SPX (represented by "X") is a function of the VIX (represented by the letter "Y") or the VIX is a function of the SPX. In case of no Granger causality, both p-values exceed the critical confidence interval of 0.05. Furthermore, "Res. DF" shows the number of observations and "Diff. DF" the number of time lags.

7.1.2.1 Period 1: 2003-2006

Figure 29 shows that between 2003 and 2006, the SPX was a function of the VIX [SPX = f(VIX)], with a lag of 1 day and a significant p-value of 3.68%. In other words, the VIX could have been used retrospectively in order to forecast the S&P 500 stock index movement.

Granger Causality Test: Y = f(X)				
Model	Res. DF	Diff. DF	F	p-value
Complete model	1003			
Reduced model	1004	-1	2.36833410772381	0.12413452084772

Granger Causality Test: X = f(Y)				
Model	Res. DF	Diff. DF	F	p-value
Complete model	1003			
Reduced model	1004	-1	4.36683544260756	0.0368964298887523

Figure 29: Granger causality test 2003-2006 (lag 1)

As a next step, this relation was re-examined, but with an increased time lag of 2 days as can be seen in

Figure 30. However, a p-value of over 12% indicates that the causal relationship is no longer present and that it is limited by a lag of one day. In other words, from 2003 until 2006 it was possible to forecast the SPX movement of tomorrow, but not the day after tomorrow.

Granger Causality Test: Y = f(X)				
Model	Res. DF	Diff. DF	F	p-value
Complete model	1000			
Reduced model	1002	-2	1.89098327031126	0.151462616109528

Granger Causality Test: X = f(Y)				
Model	Res. DF	Diff. DF	F	p-value
Complete model	1000			
Reduced model	1002	-2	2.10961088597836	0.121824608154324

Figure 30: Granger causality test 2003-2006 (lag 2)

7.1.2.2 Period 2: 2007-2008

From 2007 until 2008 there was no Granger causal relationship found, with p-values of 84% and 83% that were far away from the critical 5% limit illustrated in Figure 31.

Granger Causality Test: Y = f(X)				
Model	Res. DF	Diff. DF	F	p-value
Complete model	500			
Reduced model	501	-1	0.0371462493267404	0.847245848131243

Granger Causality Test: X = f(Y)				
Model	Res. DF	Diff. DF	F	p-value
Complete model	500			
Reduced model	501	-1	0.0459245620835621	0.830400354012398

Figure 31: Granger causality test 2007-2008

7.1.2.3 Period 3: 2009-2013

Finally, for the last period between 2009 and 2013 it was found that there was no Granger causal relationship either, but interestingly the p-values moved back closer to the critical percentage mark.

Granger Causality Test: Y = f(X)				
Model	Res. DF	Diff. DF	F	p-value
Complete model	1254			
Reduced model	1255	-1	0.087744736026162	0.76711312492137

Granger Causality Test: X = f(Y)				
Model	Res. DF	Diff. DF	F	p-value
Complete model	1254			
Reduced model	1255	-1	0.664843120611584	0.41501016468466

Figure 32: Granger causality test 2009-2013

In conclusion, the Granger causality test showed that there definitely was a statistically significant causal relationship observable between the SPX and the VIX Index from 2003 until 2006, using a time lag of one day. In other words, during this period the VIX Granger caused the S&P 500 stock index of tomorrow. However, as was already mentioned, the forecastability was no longer observable when the time lag was increased to two days. Furthermore, there was no lag-1 causality detectable during the other two time periods. Nevertheless, the p-values for all time lags and for all periods were computed in order to find potential outliers and the obtained results are illustrated in Table 6.

p-Values for Different Time Lags												
		Lags from 1-11 days and the related p-values										
Causality	**Period**	**1**	**2**	**3**	**4**	**5**	**6**	**7**	**8**	**9**	**10**	**11**
X = f(Y)	2003 - 2006	0,04	0,12	0,24	0,39	0,54	0,66	0,74	0,78	0,87	0,92	0,78
	2007 - 2008	0,83	0,91	0,89	0,78	0,91	0,95	0,92	0,90	0,94	0,76	0,71
	2009 - 2013	0,42	0,70	0,52	0,17	0,13	0,09	0,08	0,09	0,14	0,16	0,13
Y = f(X)	2003 - 2006	0,12	0,15	0,30	0,50	0,61	0,77	0,81	0,90	0,93	0,89	0,93
	2007 - 2008	0,85	0,98	0,99	0,82	0,58	0,68	0,55	0,47	0,50	0,29	0,37
	2009 - 2013	0,77	0,61	0,57	0,65	0,09	0,13	0,07	0,11	0,10	0,09	0,14

Table 6: p-values for different time lags (own table)

It is observable that there is no other time lag that results in a statistically significant causality relation in any time period. The fact that this relationship was explicitly found in one out of three observation periods indicates that the causal relationship between the two indexes is obviously unstable over time. Finally, Figure 33 summarizes the obtained research findings from the quantitative analysis.

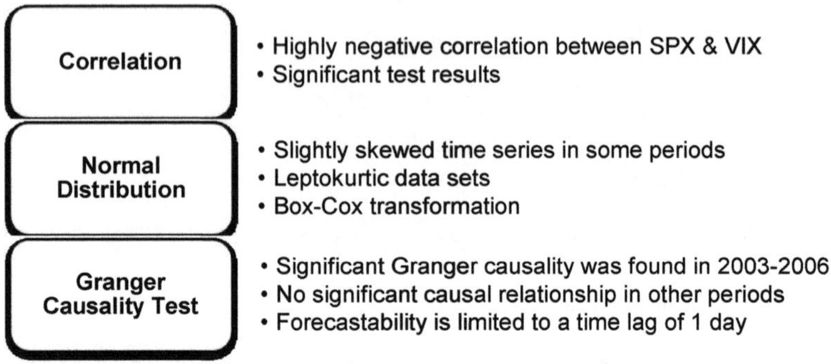

Figure 33: Quantitative research findings (own figure)

In the following chapter, the obtained findings of the qualitative research are being presented.

7.2 Qualitative Research

As mentioned in the methodological chapter, three interviews were conducted with Austrian bank industry experts. In the following paragraphs, the outcomes of the expert interviews will be presented, starting with the relevance of the VIX as a source of information and how it influences financial decision-making. Following this, awareness regarding the critique of the VIX Index will be addressed including potential alternatives, followed by the topic of behavioural finance. Finally, the causal relationship between the SPX and the VIX was discussed with the interview partners.

The first issue discussed with the interviewees addressed the relevance of the VIX in their daily business and how the VIX is used as a source of information regarding financial market volatility. It was found that the VIX itself does not play an important role in financial decision-making. One interview partner for instance, mentioned that the VIX is assumed to be a soft-fact, in other words it is characterised by subjective information and has no quantitative significance in the decision processes. Another expert confirmed the rather low relevance of the VIX by saying that the VIX and its recent development over time influences only by 5% his decision-making. Additionally, it was argued that the importance of the VIX Index might be higher for investors who own large positions in US stocks and stock options. In contrast, investors with European shares only will not pay as much attention to the volatility index. In other words, the VIX Index is just one piece of a puzzle among many, but it was added that the relevance of the VIX

"The VIX is just a soft-fact that offers subjective information".

as an information provider may depend on the current situation of the market and the asset allocation of an investor. To be precise, volatility and specifically the VIX, play a more essential role when the markets are experiencing a downturn or even a financial recession. According to industry experts, volatility management in general is more critical when nervousness in financial markets is rather high or at least getting higher, and is less interesting in times of a calm and optimistic atmosphere. Regarding the applications of the VIX it was mentioned that it is used to evaluate the financial market environment and condition. In doing so, the historical development of the VIX, VXO and implied volatility are observed and interpreted in order to estimate the nervousness in the market. Concerning the time horizon of this retrospective assessment, the answers differed greatly, ranging from until one year into the past to the whole history of the indexes. Moreover, the current level of the VIX value itself does not have any significance for the interviewees due to the fact that a rather high VIX does not necessarily mean that volatility will be a problematic issue in the upcoming weeks, especially when the VIX recently moved downwards. As a consequence, quantitative thresholds are not used in investment decisions.

The interview partner had almost no knowledge concerning the criticism and the weaknesses of the VIX Index. It was argued that due to the fact that the VIX does not significantly influence investment decisions it is sufficient to understand the meaning behind the VIX. It is also not supposed to be necessary to deal with the computation formula from a scientific perspective, because as already mentioned, the VIX is assumed to be just a soft-fact. The interviewees were also asked to think about alternatives that are used to determine market nervousness or future market volatility. In this case, the German Volatility Index (VDAX), the CSFB and the current prices of put options were mentioned. The VDAX is the German counterpart of the VIX Index and measures volatility implied by call and put option prices that are based on the German stock market index as the underlying (Wagner and Szimayer 2001). The CSFB was designed to measure investment sentiment by tracking the willingness of investors to pay up for downward protection with collar trades on the SPX option prices (Frankel 2009). Furthermore, it was noted that derivative products such as VIX options and futures are not yet being used in those banks where the interviewees are employed. Volatility and specifically the VIX is seen as a source of information about the market situation which has little influence in investment decision-making, but there is no direct exposure to volatility. In other words, benefiting from diversification effects and hedging against market volatility is not the aim.

According to the interviewed experts, much importance is already attached to the topic of behavioural finance and in their experience it is even gaining in relevance over time. In one bank there is even a behavioural finance project running in order to analyse behavioural aspects in decision-making processes. Furthermore, sentiment barometers are frequently used for market assessment purposes, but two of the interviewees added that the level of influence of behavioural finance depends not only on the current market situation, but also on the time horizon. First, during economic downturns behavioral finance enjoys more importance compared to periods of economic upturns and second, for short-time investment periods the influence is generally assumed to be higher because every news announcement is carefully weighed. For longer investment periods on the other hand, the influence seems to be lower due to the fact that then fundamentals are more important.

Regarding the forecastability of future volatility all interviewees had the same opinion, namely that this is not at all possible and that nobody and no forecasting model can achieve that. There were many arguments that were mentioned to support this theory, such as the fact that external factors such as natural catastrophes can have a huge influence on the global financial markets. Due to globalization and the resulting interconnectedness of financial markets, bankruptcies or financial scandals can affect financial markets over all continents. It was also mentioned that thus, the tail risk has increased over the last decades and is already considered to be high. Furthermore, an interviewee argued that mathematical models are still not advanced and sophisticated enough to forecast such a complex issue as future market volatility. Concerning the question whether they estimate future volatility using any forecasting model, the answers were similar from all participants. None of them tries to predict future volatility because as it was mentioned earlier, market volatility is only of real relevance in the case of market downturns and not when investors are optimistic. To be precise, more attention is paid to volatility when evaluating single stock and stock options or futures. Regarding volatility in financial markets in general, the assessment is carried out rather subjectively by estimating the current market situation. However, although others might argue that subjective interpretation cannot outperform mathematical models, the interviewees asserted that very often, decisions based on common sense and gut feeling may provide better outcomes. One expert argued that in the finance industry, the trend of over-modelling is getting ridiculously popular and the complexity of the financial markets cannot be simplified by any mathematical model. As a consequence, the interviewees also affirmed, the causal relationship between the SPX and the VIX cannot be assumed to be linear. Hypothetical arguments such as "the VIX Index Granger causes the S&P 500" or "the S&P 500 Granger causes the VIX Index" would not be confirmed in reality.

"It is not possible to forecast future volatility, nobody can do that".

Finally, Figure 34 summarizes the outcomes of the qualitative analysis for each of the main topics discussed with the industry experts.

Volatility Forecastability

- Too many external factors to forecast
- Increase of tail-risk
- Over-modelling (gut feeling & common sense)

Behavioral Finance

- Increasing relevance
- Sentiment indicators
- More relevance for short-term time horizon

VIX Relevance

- Minor role for Austrian practitioners
- Soft-fact
- More important in times of market downturns

VIX Critique

- No knowledge regarding the weaknesses
- No dealing with potential weaknesses

VIX Alternatives

- VDAX
- CSFB
- Level of put option prices

8 Discussion

As already mentioned in a preceding chapter, controversial research results were obtained from the quantitative analysis across the observed periods. Whereas in the first period from 2003 until 2006 a statistically significant Granger causal relationship was detectable, it was not the case in the following years between 2007 and 2013. Unfortunately, the distinction between economic crisis and economic boom, that was considered when framing the time horizons of the analysed periods, does not provide an explanation for the unstable causality, because in such a case, the VIX would also have caused the SPX in the last periods. As a consequence, the causal relationship between the two indexes is declared as being non-linear and unstable over time. A potential explanation for this instability may be that there is another/are other variable(s) that interfere with the linear relationship in certain market conditions, causing interruptions in the causal relationship between the SPX and the VIX Index. This assumption is confirmed by the expert interviews that have shown that there seem to be more variables or external factors that have an influence on this relationship. As a result, there must be a distinction within the different periods when answering the first research question regarding the causal relationship.

RQ 1: *Does the VIX Granger cause the S&P 500 movement or vice-versa?*

During the second and the last period from 2007 until 2013, no causality was detectable which was illustrated in Figure 31 and Figure 32. Consequently, the null hypothesis H0 was confirmed but for the first period between 2003 and 2006 a Granger causal relationship was definitely found. Therefore, the null hypothesis was rejected and due to the fact that the causality was not reciprocal, only the alternative hypothesis HA was accepted. In summary, the VIX Index caused the S&P 500 stock index between January 2003 and December 2006 which means, in other words, that the VIX could have been used in order to predict the future SPX movements.

RQ 2: *Are the future changes of the S&P 500 and/or the VIX predictable?*

Considering the observed instability of the causal relationship it is difficult to generalize the results obtained in the first period in such a way that research question number two could be confirmed. With the benefit of hindsight, the VIX could have been used to forecast the SPX movements between 2003 and 2006, but a continuation of that procedure could have caused severe consequences in the following years. As a consequence, the predictability of the future changes of the SPX and/or the VIX Index is rejected. In other words, due to the fact that no causal relationship was found between the SPX and the VIX, the research findings of this study will not have a revolutionary effect on the daily business of fund managers and risk managers.

As was mentioned by the interviewed industry experts, however, the tail risk is getting larger and therefore, the author proposes to use a confidence interval of 0.99 (1%) when calculating the Value at Risk for risk management purposes. In doing so, the tail risks that are associated with external factors will be minimized.

RQ 3: ***What are the main contradictions and similarities between volatility forecasting and volatility management in theory and practice?***

First of all, the main outcomes of the descriptive analysis are consistent with the existing literature. In particular, it was proven that the log-returns of the SPX are leptokurtic and not normally distributed. In general, there is not only a high level of controversy within the existing literature, but also some contradiction between the reviewed literature and practitioners' opinions. In research there is a general agreement that volatility is definitely forecastable to a certain degree, although the strength and decay of the predictive performance depend on factors such as data frequency and forecasting time horizon. Regarding the latter, it could be confirmed that volatility forecastability decays quickly with an increasing time horizon as was reported by Bollerslev et al. (1992). To be precise, the predictability of the future SPX movements vanished already after an increase of the time lag from one to two days. In other words, in this research it was shown that the forecastability of future SPX movement decays faster than was expected considering the existing literature.

Most interestingly, it was argued by the interviewed bank industry experts that volatility is not at all forecastable, independent of a person's know-how or model that is applied. It was mentioned that there are too many external factors that have an influence on financial market volatility and that the tail risk gets larger. This is confirmed by the existing literature, namely by the proven existence of a volatility smile and fat-tails. In addition, there are a few facts that were discovered during the qualitative interviews that allow scrutinizing the relevance of volatility forecasting that was highlighted by several surveys in the introduction of this paper.

First, the consideration of the VIX as a soft-fact that simply provides information regarding the current state of the market and the minor relevance of the VIX level in financial deci sion-making are inconsistent with the importance that is assigned to the VIX in existing literature. As was already explained in the literature review, the VIX Index is an asymmetric barometer that overemphasizes economic downturns and underestimates periods of economic growth. Although the analysis of this connection was not the aim of this research, a relation can nevertheless be established between this fact and the outcome of the qualitative findings. During an interview it was mentioned that the VIX Index plays a more important role for the evaluation of the economy in times of economic downturns. By considering the following three facts, namely that the VIX is considered to be a soft fact providing information regarding market nervousness, the asymmetry of the VIX and the

VIX's higher relevance during economic crisis, it can be assumed that market nervousness is overestimated in times of economic downturns.

Secondly, the negative correlation between the SPX and the VIX Index was confirmed by this research, which can be categorized as a similarity between the existing literature and the obtained research findings. Nevertheless, there seems to be no active trading of volatility as an underlying in Austrian banks and consequently, neither direct insurance against financial market volatility nor diversification benefits from the negative correlation can be achieved.

Thirdly, the qualitative interviews have shown that there is no knowledge or active dealing regarding the weaknesses of the VIX from a scientific perspective. It was argued that it is sufficient to understand the meaning of the index and there was no need to analyse its computation. This refusal to assess the VIX Index from a critical standpoint leads to the conclusion that bank mangers blindly trust in an index without challenging its formation.

Finally, the qualitative research results have shown that behavioral finance enjoys increasing relevance in the Austrian bank industry. To be precise, behavioral finance is assumed to have more influence on investors' decisions in times of economic downturns and when the investment time horizon is rather short. In such situations market participants should consequently observe sentiment indicators and volatility indexes including the VIX and the CSFB. Furthermore, there was agreement among the interviewed industry experts about the fact that rationality of investors seems to be limited.

9 Conclusion

The objective of this research was to analyse the weaknesses and critical opinions regarding volatility forecastability and in particular the performance of the VIX Index. In addition, the empirical part aimed at contributing to the existing literature of volatility forecasting by examining the causal relationship between the S&P 500 stock market index and the VIX Index. As a consequence, the forecastability of future SPX and VIX Index movements should be explored by considering the observed Granger causal relationship. Furthermore, the influence of behavioral finance on price movements and volatility was assessed.

According to the existing literature, future volatility is definitely predictable to a certain degree, whereupon the forecasting strength depends mostly on the chosen forecasting horizon and the data frequency. In general, the strength of forecasts can be improved by decreasing the time horizon and shortening the data frequency, but this statement is in clear contrast to the results obtained from the interviews with Austrian bank industry experts, who claimed that neither volatility nor future index movements are predictable at all, no matter which mathematical model is applied. However, the findings from the Granger causality do not indicate that future index movements are predictable. To be precise, the period between 2003 and 2006 was the only one where a Granger causal relationship was observed, at which the forecastability was limited to a time lag of one day. This confirms the forecastability decay presented in former research, although the speed of decay is even higher in this study. In the other periods from 2007 until 2013 no causal relationship was found. As a result, the instability of Granger causality over time does not lead to conclusion that the future movements of the SPX and the VIX Index are predictable, neither their direction nor the magnitude.

Regarding the weaknesses and critique of the VIX Index, there is a high level of controversy. Many researchers argue that it is a weak forecast of future short-term volatility because it is based on computation assumptions that result in a biased VIX level. Furthermore, some critics refer to a better performing volatility index such as the CSFB. Most interestingly, according to the interviewed experts, the VIX only plays a minor role anyway for financial decision-making and is considered to be a soft-fact. This is in clear contrast to the existing literature where the VIX is often praised for being an important investor fear gauge. Furthermore, the findings obtained from the interviews confirmed the increasing relevance of behavioral finance.

Concerning the potential opportunities for further research, it would be of interest to test the causal relationship between the VIX and the SPX using high-frequency data, for instance hourly or minute-by-minute log-returns instead of daily changes. In doing so, the behavioural aspect that is supposed to be greater for intraday trading, according to the experts interviewed, could be addressed more intensely. As already mentioned, the qualitative research has shown that there are many external factors which have an influence on the level of the SPX and the VIX Index. Hence, there may be (an) additional variable(s) that should be considered, such as for instance, using a Vector Autoregression approach. Concerning the qualitative analysis, research findings could vary slightly when including interview partners from a variety of countries. Finally, the industry experts argued that the VIX might be more relevant for practitioners in the US and as a consequence, there may be additional information that could be obtained by diversifying the interviewee sample. Finally, the number of interviews could also be increased when conducting further research.

Appendix

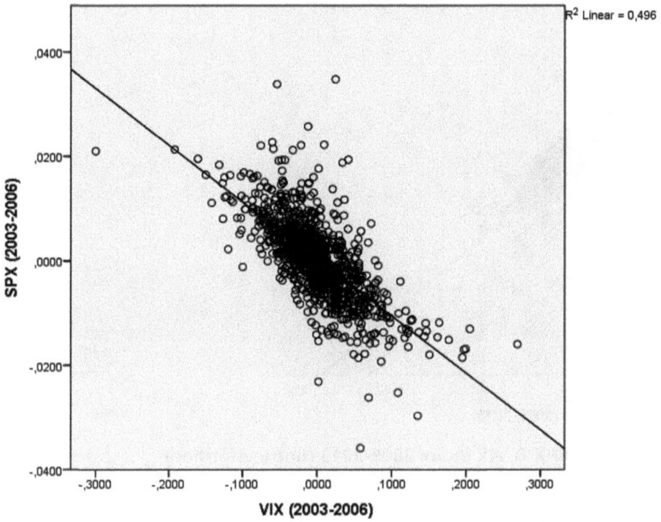

Figure 35: Correlation between SPX & VIX Index 2003-2006 (untransformed)

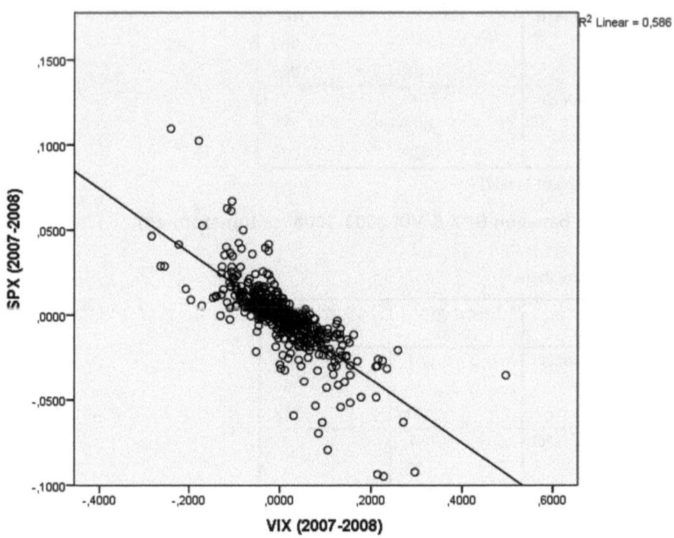

Figure 36: Correlation between SPX & VIX Index 2007-2008 (untransformed)

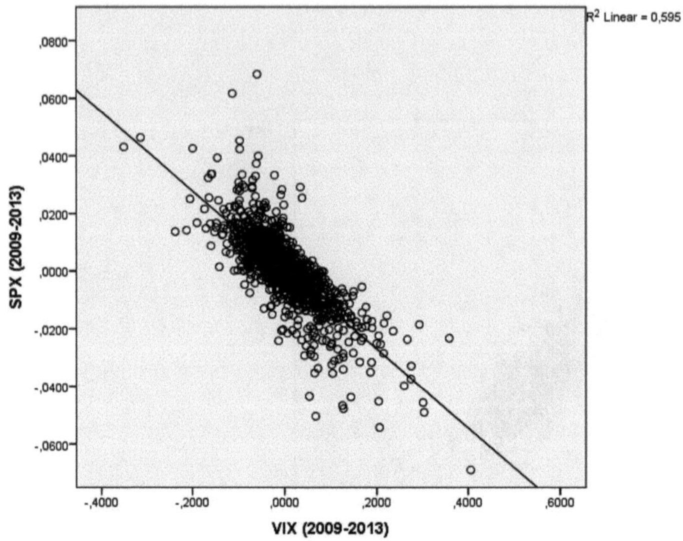

Figure 37: Correlation between SPX & VIX Index 2009-2013 (untransformed)

Correlations

		SPX (2003-2006)	VIX (2003-2006)
SPX (2003-2006)	Pearson Correlation	1	-,704**
	Sig. (2-tailed)		,000
	N	1006	1006
VIX (2003-2006)	Pearson Correlation	-,704**	1
	Sig. (2-tailed)	,000	
	N	1006	1006

**. Correlation is significant at the 0.01 level (2-tailed).

Figure 38: Pearson Correlation between SPX & VIX 2003-2006 (untransformed)

Correlations

		SPX (2007-2008)	VIX (2007-2008)
SPX (2007-2008)	Pearson Correlation	1	-,765**
	Sig. (2-tailed)		,000
	N	503	503
VIX (2007-2008)	Pearson Correlation	-,765**	1
	Sig. (2-tailed)	,000	
	N	503	503

**. Correlation is significant at the 0.01 level (2-tailed).

Figure 39: Pearson Correlation between SPX & VIX 2007-2008 (untransformed)

Correlations

		SPX (2009-2013)	VIX (2009-2013)
SPX (2009-2013)	Pearson Correlation	1	-,772**
	Sig. (2-tailed)		,000
	N	1257	1257
VIX (2009-2013)	Pearson Correlation	-,772**	1
	Sig. (2-tailed)	,000	
	N	1257	1257

**. Correlation is significant at the 0.01 level (2-tailed).

Figure 40: Pearson Correlation between SPX & VIX 2009-2013 (untransformed)

Granger Causality Test: Y = f(X)				
Model	Res.DF	Diff. DF	F	p-value
Complete model	1003			
Reduced model	1004	-1	2.36833410772381	0.12413452084772

Granger Causality Test: X = f(Y)				
Model	Res.DF	Diff. DF	F	p-value
Complete model	1003			
Reduced model	1004	-1	4.36683544260756	0.0368964298887523

Figure 41: Granger causality test 2003-2006 (lag 1)

Granger Causality Test: Y = f(X)				
Model	Res.DF	Diff. DF	F	p-value
Complete model	1000			
Reduced model	1002	-2	1.89098327031126	0.151462616109528

Granger Causality Test: X = f(Y)				
Model	Res.DF	Diff. DF	F	p-value
Complete model	1000			
Reduced model	1002	-2	2.10961088597836	0.121824608154324

Figure 42: Granger causality test 2003-2006 (lag 2)

Granger Causality Test: Y = f(X)				
Model	Res.DF	Diff. DF	F	p-value
Complete model	997			
Reduced model	1000	-3	1.23042094669216	0.297392085641341

Granger Causality Test: X = f(Y)				
Model	Res.DF	Diff. DF	F	p-value
Complete model	997			
Reduced model	1000	-3	1.40055688264812	0.241168676790646

Figure 43: Granger causality test 2003-2006 (lag 3)

Granger Causality Test: Y = f(X)				
Model	Res.DF	Diff. DF	F	p-value
Complete model	994			
Reduced model	998	-4	0.839395722280214	0.500219281836711

Granger Causality Test: X = f(Y)				
Model	Res.DF	Diff. DF	F	p-value
Complete model	994			
Reduced model	998	-4	1.03074511798454	0.390194409442036

Figure 44: Granger causality test 2003-2006 (lag 4)

Granger Causality Test: Y = f(X)				
Model	Res.DF	Diff. DF	F	p-value
Complete model	991			
Reduced model	996	-5	0.716902881066012	0.610798657406014

Granger Causality Test: X = f(Y)				
Model	Res.DF	Diff. DF	F	p-value
Complete model	991			
Reduced model	996	-5	0.808147705480896	0.543868988390745

Figure 45: Granger causality test 2003-2006 (lag 5)

Granger Causality Test: Y = f(X)				
Model	Res.DF	Diff. DF	F	p-value
Complete model	988			
Reduced model	994	-6	0.550704757826877	0.769655868517055

Granger Causality Test: X = f(Y)				
Model	Res.DF	Diff. DF	F	p-value
Complete model	988			
Reduced model	994	-6	0.686859555101267	0.660318932561363

Figure 46: Granger causality test 2003-2006 (lag 6)

Granger Causality Test: Y = f(X)				
Model	Res.DF	Diff. DF	F	p-value
Complete model	985			
Reduced model	992	-7	0.53223222150616	0.810516334273049

Granger Causality Test: X = f(Y)				
Model	Res.DF	Diff. DF	F	p-value
Complete model	985			
Reduced model	992	-7	0.617003836697249	0.742208862154166

Figure 47: Granger causality test 2003-2006 (lag 7)

Granger Causality Test: Y = f(X)				
Model	Res.DF	Diff. DF	F	p-value
Complete model	982			
Reduced model	990	-8	0.43626586410537	0.899610610261327

Granger Causality Test: X = f(Y)				
Model	Res.DF	Diff. DF	F	p-value
Complete model	982			
Reduced model	990	-8	0.598959480544231	0.779286236429676

Figure 48: Granger causality test 2003-2006 (lag 8)

Granger Causality Test: Y = f(X)				
Model	Res.DF	Diff. DF	F	p-value
Complete model	979			
Reduced model	988	-9	0.40416515283048	0.933261258239007

Granger Causality Test: X = f(Y)				
Model	Res.DF	Diff. DF	F	p-value
Complete model	979			
Reduced model	988	-9	0.506375166503848	0.870616989669691

Figure 49: Granger causality test 2003-2006 (lag 9)

Granger Causality Test: Y = f(X)				
Model	Res.DF	Diff. DF	F	p-value
Complete model	976			
Reduced model	986	-10	0.497462547833867	0.892357428908137

Granger Causality Test: X = f(Y)				
Model	Res.DF	Diff. DF	F	p-value
Complete model	976			
Reduced model	986	-10	0.453574267280378	0.919502563911249

Figure 50: Granger causality test 2003-2006 (lag 10)

Granger Causality Test: Y = f(X)				
Model	Res.DF	Diff. DF	F	p-value
Complete model	973			
Reduced model	984	-11	0.463820027157008	0.925611753538274

Granger Causality Test: X = f(Y)				
Model	Res.DF	Diff. DF	F	p-value
Complete model	973			
Reduced model	984	-11	0.648398098402742	0.78770343471525

Figure 51: Granger causality test 2003-2006 (lag 11)

Granger Causality Test: Y = f(X)				
Model	Res.DF	Diff. DF	F	p-value
Complete model	500			
Reduced model	501	-1	0.0371462493267404	0.847245848131243

Granger Causality Test: X = f(Y)				
Model	Res.DF	Diff. DF	F	p-value
Complete model	500			
Reduced model	501	-1	0.0459245620835621	0.830400354012398

Figure 52: Granger causality test 2007-2008 (lag 1)

Granger Causality Test: Y = f(X)				
Model	Res.DF	Diff. DF	F	p-value
Complete model	497			
Reduced model	499	-2	0.020491000353254	0.979718341197128

Granger Causality Test: X = f(Y)				
Model	Res.DF	Diff. DF	F	p-value
Complete model	497			
Reduced model	499	-2	0.0910064007777193	0.913027078025759

Figure 53: Granger causality test 2007-2008 (lag 2)

Granger Causality Test: Y = f(X)				
Model	Res.DF	Diff. DF	F	p-value
Complete model	494			
Reduced model	497	-3	0.0121803102043321	0.998159812534635

Granger Causality Test: X = f(Y)				
Model	Res.DF	Diff. DF	F	p-value
Complete model	494			
Reduced model	497	-3	0.206329769706145	0.892016946545712

Figure 54: Granger causality test 2007-2008 (lag 3)

Granger Causality Test: Y = f(X)				
Model	Res.DF	Diff. DF	F	p-value
Complete model	491			
Reduced model	495	-4	0.387475683262309	0.81764043962141

Granger Causality Test: X = f(Y)				
Model	Res.DF	Diff. DF	F	p-value
Complete model	491			
Reduced model	495	-4	0.4351244112118	0.783265539250833

Figure 55: Granger causality test 2007-2008 (lag 4)

Granger Causality Test: Y = f(X)				
Model	Res.DF	Diff. DF	F	p-value
Complete model	488			
Reduced model	493	-5	0.749342702305647	0.586851394006314

Granger Causality Test: X = f(Y)				
Model	Res.DF	Diff. DF	F	p-value
Complete model	488			
Reduced model	493	-5	0.311989742445945	0.905777383247894

Figure 56: Granger causality test 2007-2008 (lag 5)

Granger Causality Test: Y = f(X)				
Model	Res.DF	Diff. DF	F	p-value
Complete model	485			
Reduced model	491	-6	0.65409397462136	0.686844818570643

Granger Causality Test: X = f(Y)				
Model	Res.DF	Diff. DF	F	p-value
Complete model	485			
Reduced model	491	-6	0.26921142053833	0.95118542583451

Figure 57: Granger causality test 2007-2008 (lag 6)

Granger Causality Test: Y = f(X)				
Model	Res.DF	Diff. DF	F	p-value
Complete model	482			
Reduced model	489	-7	0.835117593849747	0.5584662585717

Granger Causality Test: X = f(Y)				
Model	Res.DF	Diff. DF	F	p-value
Complete model	482			
Reduced model	489	-7	0.37168890735534	0.918727034062917

Figure 58: Granger causality test 2007-2008 (lag 7)

Granger Causality Test: Y = f(X)				
Model	Res.DF	Diff. DF	F	p-value
Complete model	479			
Reduced model	487	-8	0.959778297178641	0.466868983207552

Granger Causality Test: X = f(Y)				
Model	Res.DF	Diff. DF	F	p-value
Complete model	479			
Reduced model	487	-8	0.429284813017726	0.903537081879839

Figure 59: Granger causality test 2007-2008 (lag 8)

Granger Causality Test: Y = f(X)				
Model	Res.DF	Diff. DF	F	p-value
Complete model	476			
Reduced model	485	-9	0.932702336317749	0.496140858572623

Granger Causality Test: X = f(Y)				
Model	Res.DF	Diff. DF	F	p-value
Complete model	476			
Reduced model	485	-9	0.388776177288746	0.940519927057883

Figure 60: Granger causality test 2007-2008 (lag 9)

Granger Causality Test: Y = f(X)				
Model	Res.DF	Diff. DF	F	p-value
Complete model	473			
Reduced model	483	-10	1.19408606780666	0.292353879234559

Granger Causality Test: X = f(Y)				
Model	Res.DF	Diff. DF	F	p-value
Complete model	473			
Reduced model	483	-10	0.663040839602347	0.758949867799244

Figure 61: Granger causality test 2007-2008 (lag 10)

Granger Causality Test: Y = f(X)				
Model	Res.DF	Diff. DF	F	p-value
Complete model	470			
Reduced model	481	-11	1.08148679496258	0.374236411853238

Granger Causality Test: X = f(Y)				
Model	Res.DF	Diff. DF	F	p-value
Complete model	470			
Reduced model	481	-11	0.731141410637018	0.708765119395772

Figure 62: Granger causality test 2007-2008 (lag 11)

Granger Causality Test: Y = f(X)				
Model	Res.DF	Diff. DF	F	p-value
Complete model	1254			
Reduced model	1255	-1	0.087744736026162	0.76711312492137

Granger Causality Test: X = f(Y)				
Model	Res.DF	Diff. DF	F	p-value
Complete model	1254			
Reduced model	1255	-1	0.664843120611584	0.41501016468466

Figure 63: Granger causality test 2009-2013 (lag 1)

Granger Causality Test: Y = f(X)				
Model	Res.DF	Diff. DF	F	p-value
Complete model	1251			
Reduced model	1253	-2	0.48937915449511	0.613124162953889

Granger Causality Test: X = f(Y)				
Model	Res.DF	Diff. DF	F	p-value
Complete model	1251			
Reduced model	1253	-2	0.363385937536779	0.695391402152172

Figure 64: Granger causality test 2009-2013 (lag 2)

Granger Causality Test: Y = f(X)				
Model	Res.DF	Diff. DF	F	p-value
Complete model	1248			
Reduced model	1251	-3	0.671392159334472	0.569638671494662

Granger Causality Test: X = f(Y)				
Model	Res.DF	Diff. DF	F	p-value
Complete model	1248			
Reduced model	1251	-3	0.746713183337084	0.524302096008303

Figure 65: Granger causality test 2009-2013 (lag 3)

Granger Causality Test: Y = f(X)				
Model	Res.DF	Diff. DF	F	p-value
Complete model	1245			
Reduced model	1249	-4	0.612841281230092	0.653445199662717

Granger Causality Test: X = f(Y)				
Model	Res.DF	Diff. DF	F	p-value
Complete model	1245			
Reduced model	1249	-4	1.61200179806184	0.168833788247483

Figure 66: Granger causality test 2009-2013 (lag 4)

Granger Causality Test: Y = f(X)				
Model	Res.DF	Diff. DF	F	p-value
Complete model	1242			
Reduced model	1247	-5	1.90947436260837	0.0899577764796481

Granger Causality Test: X = f(Y)				
Model	Res.DF	Diff. DF	F	p-value
Complete model	1242			
Reduced model	1247	-5	1.70715683663749	0.129957904720173

Figure 67: Granger causality test 2009-2013 (lag 5)

Granger Causality Test: Y = f(X)				
Model	Res.DF	Diff. DF	F	p-value
Complete model	1239			
Reduced model	1245	-6	1.63426048815475	0.134105771145612

Granger Causality Test: X = f(Y)				
Model	Res.DF	Diff. DF	F	p-value
Complete model	1239			
Reduced model	1245	-6	1.8200808179831	0.0918308185437005

Figure 68: Granger causality test 2009-2013 (lag 6)

Granger Causality Test: Y = f(X)				
Model	Res.DF	Diff. DF	F	p-value
Complete model	1236			
Reduced model	1243	-7	1.85724467358253	0.0731152712117708

Granger Causality Test: X = f(Y)				
Model	Res.DF	Diff. DF	F	p-value
Complete model	1236			
Reduced model	1243	-7	1.84235574683528	0.07570619176569

Figure 69: Granger causality test 2009-2013 (lag 7)

Granger Causality Test: Y = f(X)				
Model	Res.DF	Diff. DF	F	p-value
Complete model	1233			
Reduced model	1241	-8	1.64818376637209	0.106880033498721

Granger Causality Test: X = f(Y)				
Model	Res.DF	Diff. DF	F	p-value
Complete model	1233			
Reduced model	1241	-8	1.70186379405553	0.0935912493538219

Figure 70: Granger causality test 2009-2013 (lag 8)

Granger Causality Test: Y = f(X)				
Model	Res.DF	Diff. DF	F	p-value
Complete model	1230			
Reduced model	1239	-9	1.6393595520527	0.0992721597124586

Granger Causality Test: X = f(Y)				
Model	Res.DF	Diff. DF	F	p-value
Complete model	1230			
Reduced model	1239	-9	1.51352691789587	0.137858437196304

Figure 71: Granger causality test 2009-2013 (lag 9)

Granger Causality Test: Y = f(X)				
Model	Res.DF	Diff. DF	F	p-value
Complete model	1227			
Reduced model	1237	-10	1.6441399041781	0.0891196952910704

Granger Causality Test: X = f(Y)				
Model	Res.DF	Diff. DF	F	p-value
Complete model	1227			
Reduced model	1237	-10	1.44375969833455	0.155514577821447

Figure 72: Granger causality test 2009-2013 (lag 10)

Granger Causality Test: Y = f(X)				
Model	Res.DF	Diff. DF	F	p-value
Complete model	1224			
Reduced model	1235	-11	1.4589668014466	0.141025582828377

Granger Causality Test: X = f(Y)				
Model	Res.DF	Diff. DF	F	p-value
Complete model	1224			
Reduced model	1235	-11	1.47785597803363	0.133559406633231

Figure 73: Granger causality test 2009-2013 (lag 11)

Source Code of R Module

```
library(lmtest)
par1 <- as.numeric(par1)
par2 <- as.numeric(par2)
par3 <- as.numeric(par3)
par4 <- as.numeric(par4)
par5 <- as.numeric(par5)
par6 <- as.numeric(par6)
par7 <- as.numeric(par7)
par8 <- as.numeric(par8)
ox <- x
oy <- y
if (par1 == 0) {
x <- log(x)
} else {
x <- (x ^ par1 - 1) / par1
}
if (par5 == 0) {
y <- log(y)
} else {
y <- (y ^ par5 - 1) / par5
}
if (par2 > 0) x <- diff(x,lag=1,difference=par2)
if (par6 > 0) y <- diff(y,lag=1,difference=par6)
if (par3 > 0) x <- diff(x,lag=par4,difference=par3)
if (par7 > 0) y <- diff(y,lag=par4,difference=par7)
x
y
(gyx <- grangertest(y ~ x, order=par8))
(gxy <- grangertest(x ~ y, order=par8))
bitmap(file="test1.png")
op <- par(mfrow=c(2,1))
(r <- ccf(ox,oy,main="Cross Correlation Function (raw data)",ylab="CCF",xlab="Lag (k)"))
(r <- ccf(x,y,main="Cross Correlation Function (transformed and differ-
enced)",ylab="CCF",xlab="Lag (k)"))
```

```
par(op)
dev.off()
bitmap(file="test2.png")
op <- par(mfrow=c(2,1))
acf(ox,lag.max=round(length(x)/2),main="ACF of x (raw)")
acf(x,lag.max=round(length(x)/2),main="ACF of x (transformed and differenced)")
par(op)
dev.off()
bitmap(file="test3.png")
op <- par(mfrow=c(2,1))
acf(oy,lag.max=round(length(y)/2),main="ACF of y (raw)")
acf(y,lag.max=round(length(y)/2),main="ACF of y (transformed and differenced)")
par(op)
dev.off()
load(file="createtable")
a<-table.start()
a<-table.row.start(a)
a<-table.element(a,"Granger Causality Test: Y = f(X)",5,TRUE)
a<-table.row.end(a)
a<-table.row.start(a)
a<-table.element(a,"Model",header=TRUE)
a<-table.element(a,"Res.DF",header=TRUE)
a<-table.element(a,"Diff. DF",header=TRUE)
a<-table.element(a,"F",header=TRUE)
a<-table.element(a,"p-value",header=TRUE)
a<-table.row.end(a)
a<-table.row.start(a)
a<-table.element(a,"Complete model",header=TRUE)
a<-table.element(a,gyx$Res.Df[1])
a<-table.element(a,"")
a<-table.element(a,"")
a<-table.element(a,"")
a<-table.row.end(a)
a<-table.row.start(a)
a<-table.element(a,"Reduced model",header=TRUE)
```

```
a<-table.element(a,gyx$Res.Df[2])
a<-table.element(a,gyx$Df[2])
a<-table.element(a,gyx$F[2])
a<-table.element(a,gyx$Pr[2])
a<-table.row.end(a)
a<-table.end(a)
table.save(a,file="mytable1.tab")
a<-table.start()
a<-table.row.start(a)
a<-table.element(a,"Granger Causality Test: X = f(Y)",5,TRUE)
a<-table.row.end(a)
a<-table.row.start(a)
a<-table.element(a,"Model",header=TRUE)
a<-table.element(a,"Res.DF",header=TRUE)
a<-table.element(a,"Diff. DF",header=TRUE)
a<-table.element(a,"F",header=TRUE)
a<-table.element(a,"p-value",header=TRUE)
a<-table.row.end(a)
a<-table.row.start(a)
a<-table.element(a,"Complete model",header=TRUE)
a<-table.element(a,gxy$Res.Df[1])
a<-table.element(a,"")
a<-table.element(a,"")
a<-table.element(a,"")
a<-table.row.end(a)
a<-table.row.start(a)
a<-table.element(a,"Reduced model",header=TRUE)
a<-table.element(a,gxy$Res.Df[2])
a<-table.element(a,gxy$Df[2])
a<-table.element(a,gxy$F[2])
a<-table.element(a,gxy$Pr[2])
a<-table.row.end(a)
a<-table.end(a)
table.save(a,file="mytable2.tab")
```

Dimension	Category	Code	Example
Volatility	Relevance	Market situation	"Volatility is more crucial in times of high investor anxiety".
		Underlying asset	"Volatility enjoys more attention when evaluating individual stocks as opposed to stock indexes".
	Forecasting	Forecastability	"Volatility is not predictable. Nobody can predict it because mathematical models are not sophisticated enough".
		External factors	"Tail risk is getting higher because there are so many unpredictable external factors like for instance natural catastrophes".
		Subjective evaluation	"Sometimes it may be better to concentrate on one's gut feeling and the common sense approach".
		Causal relationship	"I do not think that one index causes the other to move because there is no linear relationship".
VIX Index	Relevance	Soft-fact	"The VIX Index is a soft-fact and consequently, rather subjective".
		Market evaluation	"We use the VIX in order to evaluate the current nervousness in financial markets".
		Derivatives	"We do not invest in derivative products such as VIX options and futures".
	Weaknesses	Awareness	"I do not have any knowledge about the weaknesses of the VIX Index...".
		Reaction	"We do not actively deal with the weaknesses of the VIX because due to the fact that it is a soft-fact there is no need to discuss it from a scientific perspective".
	Alternatives	Volatility indexes	"We look at the VDAX and the CSFB...".
		Option prices	"I observe the price development of put options...".
Behavioural Finance	Relevance	Trend	"Behavioural finance enjoys increasing relevance…".
		Sentiment	"We follow sentiment indicators in order to evaluate the nervousness of investors".
	Level of influence	Time horizon	"For short-time periods behavioural finance is more relevant in my opinion and for long-time periods it seems to be less important because…".
		Market situation	"When financial markets are nervous behavioural finance has more influence on investment decisions compared to…".

Table 7: Coding template

10 List of References

Adrian, T. & N. Boyarchenko. 2012. Intermediary leverage cycles and financial stability. Staff Report, Federal Reserve Bank of New York.

Ahn, C., S. Byoun & H. Y. Park. 2003. Put-Call Parity: The Case of KOSPI 200 Options in Korea. working paper.

Andersen, T. G. (2000) Some reflections on analysis of high-frequency data. *Journal of Business & Economic Statistics,* 18, 146-153.

Baba, N. & Y. Sakurai (2011) Predicting regime switches in the VIX index with macroeconomic variables. *Applied Economics Letters,* 18, 1415-1419.

Bakshi, G. & N. Kapadia (2003) Delta-hedged gains and the negative market volatility risk premium. *Review of Financial Studies,* 16, 527-566.

Becker, R., A. E. Clements & A. McClelland (2009) The jump component of S&P 500 volatility and the VIX index. *Journal of Banking & Finance,* 33, 1033-1038.

Beckers, S. (1981) Standard deviations implied in option prices as predictors of future stock price variability. *Journal of Banking & Finance,* 5, 363-381.

Bharadwaj, A. & J. B. Wiggins (2001) Box spread and put-call parity tests for the S&P 500 index LEAPS market. *The Journal of Derivatives,* 8, 62-71.

Bilello, C. 2014. Brace Yourself For a More Volatile Stock Market. money.usnews.com.

Bittman, J. (2007) VIX: It protects and diversifies. *FUTURES-CEDAR FALLS IOWA THEN CHICAGO-,* 36, 38.

Black, F. (1986) Noise. *The journal of finance,* 41, 529-543.

Blenman, L. P. & G. J. Wang (2012) New Insights on the Implied and Realized Volatility Relation. *Review of Pacific Basin Financial Markets and Policies,* 15.

Bollerslev, T. (1986) Generalized autoregressive conditional heteroskedasticity. *Journal of econometrics,* 31, 307-327.

Bollerslev, T., R. Y. Chou & K. F. Kroner (1992) ARCH modeling in finance: A review of the theory and empirical evidence. *Journal of econometrics,* 52, 5-59.

Bondt, W. F. & R. Thaler (1985) Does the stock market overreact? *The Journal of finance,* 40, 793-805.

Box, G. E. & D. R. Cox (1964) An analysis of transformations. *Journal of the Royal Statistical Society, Series B,* 26, 211-252.

Brunnermeier, M. K. & Y. Sannikov (2012) A macroeconomic model with a financial sector.

Bryman, A. 2012. *Social research methods.* Oxford university press.

Canina, L. & S. Figlewski (1993) The informational content of implied volatility. *Review of Financial studies,* 6, 659-681.

Carr, P. & L. Wu (2004) A tale of two indices.

Cavalheiro, E. A., K. M. Vieira, P. S. Ceretta, L. De Lima Trindade & C. E. M. Tavares (2011) Misattribution Bias: The Role of Emotion in Risk Tolerance. *IUP Journal of Behavioral Finance,* 8.

CBOE. 2014a. The CBOE Volatility Index An Introduction to the VIX Index. CBOE.com: CBOE.

CBOE. 2014b. Negative Correlations of Daily Returns of VIX vs. S&P 500. CBOE.com: CBOE.

CBOE. 2014c. (VIX) Volatility S&P 500. cboe.com: Chicago Boards of Options Exchange.

Chen, A.-S. (1997) Forecasting the S&P 500 index volatility. *International Review of Economics & Finance,* 6, 391-404.

Christensen, B. J. & N. R. Prabhala (1998) The relation between implied and realized volatility. *Journal of Financial Economics,* 50, 125-150.

Christoffersen, P. F. & F. X. Diebold (2000) How relevant is volatility forecasting for financial risk management? *Review of Economics and Statistics,* 82, 12-22.

Cipollini, A. & A. Manzini (2007) Can the VIX signal market's direction? An asymmetric dynamic strategy. *An Asymmetric Dynamic Strategy (April 2007).*

Cornell, B., W. Landsman & S. Stubben (2011) Do Institutional Investors and Security Analysts Mitigate the Effects of Investor Sentiment? *Available at SSRN 1848207.*

Daigler, R. T. & L. Rossi (2006) A portfolio of stocks and volatility. *The Journal of Investing,* 15, 99-106.

Dash, S. & M. T. Moran (2005) VIX as a companion for hedge fund portfolios. *The Journal of Alternative Investments,* 8, 75-80.

De Bondt, W., G. Muradoglu, H. Shefrin & S. K. Staikouras (2008) Behavioral finance: Quo vadis? *Journal of Applied Finance,* 18, 7-21.

De Bondt, W. F. & R. H. Thaler (1987) Further evidence on investor overreaction and stock market seasonality. *Journal of finance*, 557-581.

Deacon, D. B. & A. Fenton (1998) N.(1998).'Collision or Collusion? A Discussion of the Unplanned Triangulation of Quantitative and Qualitative Research Methods'. *International Journal of Social Research Methodology,* 1, 47-63.

Deng, G., C. McCann & O. Wang (2012) Are VIX Futures ETPs Effective Hedges? *The Journal of Index Investing,* 3, 35-48.

Denzin, N. K. (1970) The research act in sociology: A theoretical introduction to sociological methods.

Dshort.com. 2014. The S&P 500 and the VIX Since 1990. Dshort.com: DShort.

Durand, R. B., M. Simon & A. Szimayer (2009) Anger, sadness and bear markets. *Applied Financial Economics,* 19, 357-369.

Ederington, L. H. & W. Guan (2002) Measuring implied volatility: is an average better? Which average? *Journal of Futures Markets,* 22, 811-837.

Ederington, L. H. & W. Guan (2006) Measuring historical volatility. *Journal of Applied Finance,* 16.

Ederington, L. H. & W. Guan (2010) Longer-Term Time-Series Volatility Forecasts.

Edmondson, A. C. & S. E. McManus (2007) Methodological fit in management field research. *Academy of management review,* 32, 1246-1264.

Engle, R. F. (1982) Autoregressive conditional heteroscedasticity with estimates of the variance of United Kingdom inflation. *Econometrica: Journal of the Econometric Society,* 987-1007.

Exchange, C. B. O. (2009) The CBOE Volatility Index - VIX. *White Paper.*

Falloon, W. (1999) Growin'Up: The big pension funds are finally waking up to the notion of VAR. *RISK-LONDON-RISK MAGAZINE LIMITED-,* 12, 26-32.

Fama, E. F. (1965) The behavior of stock-market prices. *Journal of business,* 34-105.

Fama, E. F. & K. R. French (1992) The cross-section of expected stock returns. *the Journal of Finance,* 47, 427-465.

Ferris, S. P., W. Kim & K. Park (2010) The informational quality of implied volatility and the volatility risk premium. *Applied Economics Letters,* 17, 445-450.

Figlewski, S. (1997) Forecasting volatility. *Financial markets, institutions & instruments,* 6, 1-88.

Fleming, J. (1998) The quality of market volatility forecasts implied by S&P 100 index option prices. *Journal of Empirical Finance,* 5, 317-345.

Fleming, J., B. Ostdiek & R. E. Whaley (1995) Predicting stock market volatility: A new measure. *Journal of Futures Markets,* 15, 265-302.

Fortune, P. (1996) Anomalies in option pricing: The black-scholes model revisited. *New England Economic Review,* 17-40.

Frankel, D. 2009. Credit Suisse Rolls Out Fear Barometer. ed. L. Adler. uk.reuters.com: uk.reuters.

French, K. R. & R. Roll (1986) Stock return variances: The arrival of information and the reaction of traders. *Journal of financial economics,* 17, 5-26.

Friedman, M. (1953) The case for flexible exchange rates.

Gençay, R., M. Dacorogna, U. A. Muller, O. Pictet & R. Olsen. 2001. *An introduction to high-frequency finance*. Academic Press.

Giot, P. (2005) Relationships between implied volatility indexes and stock index returns. *The Journal of Portfolio Management,* 31, 92-100.

Grable, J. E. & M. J. Roszkowski (2008) The influence of mood on the willingness to take financial risks. *Journal of Risk Research,* 11, 905-923.

Grossman, S. J. & J. E. Stiglitz (1980) On the impossibility of informationally efficient markets. *The American economic review*, 393-408.

Harris, L. 2002. *Trading and exchanges: Market microstructure for practitioners.* Oxford University Press.

Howard, C. T. (2013) Behavioral Portfolio Management. *Available at SSRN 2210032.*

Hull, J. C. 2012. *Risk Management and Financial Institutions.* New Jersey and Canada: John Wiley & Sons, Inc.

Jackwerth, J. C. & M. Rubinstein (1996) Recovering probability distributions from option prices. *The Journal of Finance,* 51, 1611-1631.

Jean-Peirre, F., G. Papanicolaou & K. R. Sircar. 2000. *Derivatives in financial markets with stochastic volatility.* Cambridge University Press.

Jiang, G. J. & Y. S. Tian (2007) Extracting model-free volatility from option prices: An examination of the VIX index. *The Journal of Derivatives,* 14, 35-60.

Jorion, P. (1995) Predicting volatility in the foreign exchange market. *The Journal of Finance,* 50, 507-528.

Kahneman, D. & A. Tversky (1973) On the psychology of prediction. *Psychological review,* 80, 237.

Kisling, W. 2010. Popular VIX Fails to Predict Stock Market Moves, Study Says. Seattle: Seattle Times.

Kritzman, M. (1991) What Practitioners Need to Know About Estimating Volatility. Part 1. *Financial Analysts Journal*, 22-25.

Kuhnen, C. M. & B. Knutson (2011) The influence of affect on beliefs, preferences, and financial decisions. *Journal of Financial and Quantitative Analysis,* 46, 605-626.

Ladd, S. 2012. Financial Volatility Ranks as Top Emerging Risk in Actuarial Study. In *Financial Executives Magazine*, 1. Financial Executives.

Laurent, S. & J.-P. Peters (2002) A tutorial for G@ RCH 2.3, a complete Ox package for estimating and forecasting ARCH models. *Journal of Economic Survey,* 4, 25-36.

Lawrence, E. R., G. McCabe & A. J. Prakash (2007) Answering financial anomalies: Sentiment-based stock pricing. *The Journal of Behavioral Finance,* 8, 161-171.

Li, C. A. & J. C. Wang (2013) THE INFLUENCES OF GREED AND FEAR ON FUND PERFORMANCE. *International Journal of Business & Finance Research (IJBFR),* 7.

Libertini, A. B. N. 2014. Overreaction Can Move Markets - And Not Just Domestically. Investment Advisor.

Loewenstein, G. F., E. U. Weber, C. K. Hsee & N. Welch (2001) Risk as feelings. *Psychological bulletin,* 127, 267.

Majmudar, U. & A. Banerjee. 2004. Vix forecasting. In *The 40th Annual Conference of the Indian Econometrics Society.*

Nwogugu, M. C. (2012) A Critique of The VIX Index, CDS Indices, Options-Based Indices, and Synthetic ETFs/Funds. *CDs Indices, Options-Based Indices, and Synthetic ETFs/Funds (March 10, 2012).*

Officer, A. J. 2009. Stock Volatility Is Down: But Is That Good News? content.time.com.

Olsen, R. A. (1998) Behavioral finance and its implications for stock-price volatility. *Financial analysts journal,* 10-18.

Parkinson, M. (1980) The extreme value method for estimating the variance of the rate of return. *Journal of Business,* 53, 61.

Poon, S.-H. 2005. *A practical guide to forecasting financial market volatility.* John Wiley & Sons.

Poon, S.-H. & C. W. Granger (2003) Forecasting volatility in financial markets: A review. *Journal of economic literature,* 41, 478-539.

Press, S. J. (1967) A compound events model for security prices. *Journal of business,* 317-335.

Rattray, S. & V. Balasubramanian (2003) The new VIX as a market signal—It still works. *Goldman Sachs Equity Derivatives Strategy.*

Ricciardi, V. (2008) The psychology of risk: The behavioral finance perspective. *Handbook of finance.*

Rizzi, J. V. (2008) Behavioral basis of the financial crisis. *Journal of Applied Finance,* 18, 84-96.

Roll, R. (1977) A critique of the asset pricing theory's tests Part I: On past and potential testability of the theory. *Journal of financial economics,* 4, 129-176.

Saldaña, J. 2012. *The coding manual for qualitative researchers.* Sage.

Sawers, A. 2012. Top Risk for Treasurers: Volatility. US: CFO.com.

Shiller, R. J. 1980. Do stock prices move too much to be justified by subsequent changes in dividends? National Bureau of Economic Research Cambridge, Mass., USA.

Shiller, (2003). From efficient markets theory to behavioral finance. *Journal of economic perspectives*, 83-104.

Shu, J. & J. E. Zhang (2003) The relationship between implied and realized volatility of S&P 500 index. *Wilmott magazine*, **4**, 83-91.

Smithson, C. & L. Minton (1996) Value-at-risk: The first of two articles on value-of-risk, outlining the different ways of calculating this popular risk measure. *RISK-LONDON-RISK MAGAZINE LIMITED-*, 9, 25-28.

Solomon, J. 2014. Get Used to Market Volatility. In *Money CNN*. CNN: CNN.

Thaler, R. H. (1999) The end of behavioral finance. *Financial Analysts Journal*, 12-17.

Toikka, M., E. Tom, S. Chadwick & M. Bolt-Christmas (2004) The Volatility Risk Premium: Sell Volatility. *CSFB Equity Derivatives Strategy-Market Commentary*, 26.

Tom, E. K. 2012. VIX Whipsaws Intraday on "Shadow" Bids for Tails. ed. C. Suisse. Market Commentary: Credit Suisse.

Turner, A. L. & E. J. Weigel (1992) Daily stock market volatility: 1928–1989. *Management Science*, 38, 1586-1609.

Wagner, D., D. M. Ellis & D. A. Dubofsky (1996) The Factors Behind Put-Call Parity Violations of S&P 100 Index Options. *Financial Review*, 31, 535-552.

Wagner, N. & A. Szimayer (2001) Alternative model specifications for implied volatility measured by the German VDAX. *Kredit und Kapital*, 34, 590-618.

Warren, G. J. (2012) Can Investing in Volatility Help Meet Your Portfolio Objectives? *The Journal of Portfolio Management*, 38, 82-98.

Wessa, P. 2013. Bivariate Granger Causality (v1.0.3) in Free Statistics Software (v1.1.23-r7). Office for Research Development and Education.

Whaley, R. E. (2008) Understanding VIX. *Available at SSRN 1296743*.

Whaley, R. E. (2009) Understanding the VIX. *The Journal of Portfolio Management*, 35, 98-105.

Whaley, R. E. (2013) Trading Volatility: At What Cost? *The Journal of Portfolio Management*, 40, 95-108.

Wintner, S. 2013. Understanding the Implications of the S&P500 Index Volatility Skew on VIX Index Changes. ed. W. Stefan. Sigmasquare.ch: Sigmasquare Capital AG.

Yahoo.Finance. 2014. Stock Volatility Likely in 2014. Australia: yahoo.finance Australia.

Yalincak, H. (2012) Criticism of the Black-Scholes Model: But Why is it Still Used?:(The Answer is Simpler than the Formula). *The Answer is Simpler than the Formula)(July 22, 2012).*

Yalinçak, H. (2012) Criticism of the Black-Scholes Model: But Why is it Still Used?:(The Answer is Simpler than the Formula). *The Answer is Simpler than the Formula)(July 22, 2012).*

Yang, D. & Q. Zhang (2000) Drift-independent volatility estimation based on high, low, open, and close prices*. *The Journal of Business,* 73, 477-492.

Zouaoui, M., G. Nouyrigat & F. Beer (2011) How does investor sentiment affect stock market crises? Evidence from panel data. *Financial Review,* 46, 723-747.

MIX
Papier aus verantwortungsvollen Quellen
Paper from responsible sources
FSC® C105338

If you have any concerns about our products,
you can contact us on
ProductSafety@springernature.com

In case Publisher is established outside the EU,
the EU authorized representative is:
Springer Nature Customer Service Center GmbH
Europaplatz 3, 69115 Heidelberg, Germany

Printed by Libri Plureos GmbH
in Hamburg, Germany